Alice Oshima . Ann Hogue

Introduction to Academic Writing

 **Addison-Wesley Publishing Company**

Reading, Massachusetts • Menlo Park, California • New York
Don Mills, Ontario • Wokingham, England • Amsterdam • Bonn • Sydney
Singapore • Tokyo • Madrid • Bogota • Santiago • San Juan

A Publication of the World Language Division

Sponsoring Editor: Kathleen Sands-Boehmer
Production/Manufacturing: James W. Gibbons
Cover Design: Dick Hannus
Production Services: Jeanine Ardourel & Associates
  Text Design: Al Burkhardt
  Illustrations: Mary Burkhardt
  Copy Editing: Lorraine Anderson
Photo Research: Merle Sciacca

Photo Credits: cover Marshall Henrichs; p. 2 Wide World Photos; p. 8 San Francisco Convention
& Visitors Bureau; p. 18 Ed Callery; p. 31 Ed Callery; p. 38 (top) State Archives, Honolulu,
Hawaii, George E. Bacon, (bottom) Hawaii State Archives; p. 40 © M.C. Escher Heirs care of
Cordon Art-Baarn-Holland; p. 54 (top) Salem High School, New Hampshire, (bottom) North-
eastern University photo by J.D. Levine; p. 72 Mary Messenger; p. 75 Ford Motor Company;
p. 82 (top) Kathy Sands-Boehmer, (bottom) Merle Sciacca; p. 86 Miami Herald photo from the
American Red Cross; p.92 Mary E. Messenger; p. 104 (top) McDonald's, (bottom) Friendly Ice
Cream Corporation; p. 126 (top) Grant Haist, (bottom) The National Tourist Office of Spain;
p. 154 (top) Wide World Photos, Inc., (bottom) Massachusetts General Hospital; p. 178 (top)
Ralph P. Turcotte, (bottom) Laurent Broussal

ISBN: 0-201-14507-3
13 14 15 16 17 18 19 20-CRS-97 96 95 94 93

Contents

Part II   Expository Writing

Introduction

Introduction to Academic Writing is an intermediate writing textbook and workbook for non-native speakers of English from age 16 through adult. It is a comprehensive writing text that uses high interest topics to teach rhetoric, grammar, and sentence structure.

This textbook contains ten chapters, each requiring 6 to 10 hours of class time. It covers a wide range of skills from basic punctuation and capitalization rules in Chapter 1 to rather advanced clause work in Chapters 8, 9, and 10. The organization is highly flexible, allowing teachers to select chapters or sections of chapters suitable for the varying abilities typical of intermediate classes.

Chapters 1–3 and 7–10 include sections on organization, grammar, and sentence structure. Chapters 4, 5, and 6 are the organization sections, in which rhetorical principles are explained and practiced at both the paragraph and essay levels. Each chapter begins with a model essay exemplifying one of the basic modes of writing: narration (temporal order), description (spatial order), and exposition (classification, comparison and contrast, and persuasion).

The grammar sections are selective rather than comprehensive; that is, they present items of grammar that are pertinent to the rhetorical modes being studied (such as comparatives in Chapter 10, Comparison and Contrast) or that are especially troublesome to intermediate learners of English (such as simple past vs. present perfect verb tense).

The sentence structure sections present three types of English sentences (simple, compound, and complex) in order of progressive difficulty. In the first three chapters, simple and compound sentences are taught and practiced extensively. Then, the structure of independent and dependent clauses is taught. The coverage in later chapters includes complex sentences with dependent adverb, noun, and adjective clauses.

Most chapters also contain a dictation/dictocomp, sentence combining exercises, a freewriting assignment, and prewriting and postwriting activities.

Each chapter concludes with a choice of writing assignments, with the more difficult ones marked with a star.

The overall organization of the book is as follows: In Chapters 1–3, students work with the "easier" modes of narration and description. The final writing assignment for these chapters can be either a single paragraph or a multiparagraph essay. In Chapter 4, a detailed examination of paragraph structure begins and continues in Chapter 5. Chapter 6 teaches basic essay organization in depth, and the remaining chapters expand on this information to include the various essay forms: classification, persuasion, etc. A chapter on business letter writing is included, as nearly all ESL/EFL students need to know the conventions of English-language business letters at some time.

Additional features of *Introduction to Academic Writing*:

- Every effort has been made to control the vocabulary. Idioms and words or expressions that may cause difficulty are marked with an asterisk and are glossed in footnotes at the bottom of the page.

- Explanations and directions are written in simple English to make it easy for students to read and understand on their own.

- Each of the grammar and sentence structure sections within a chapter are independent and, therefore, are optional. A section may be omitted if the teacher judges it to be too elementary or too advanced for his or her class. Omitted sections may, of course, be assigned to individual students for remedial/supplemental work as needed.

- Prewriting (brainstorming, outlining, draft writing) and postwriting (drafts, checklists) activities are interspersed throughout the text.

To the Teacher

The following paragraphs present explanations and suggestions for the activities in *Introduction to Academic Writing*, as well as additional information that may be helpful.

Dictation / Dictocomp Practices.

Dictocomps are usually short paragraphs that reflect the rhetoric, grammar, and sentence structure elements of each chapter. You may use these exercises as traditional dictations or you may use them as dictocomps, whichever best fits your teaching style. For the traditional dictation technique, assign the material for study; then, in class, ask the students to transcribe the material as you dictate it. For the dictocomp technique, present the material as an unannounced in-class composition exercise toward the end of the class's study of the chapter.

The dictocomp method is simple: read the material (usually a paragraph) two or three times to the class. Do not permit the class to take notes during the readings. You then may answer questions after the readings, or, alternatively, may solicit a verbal recitation of the material. Write any difficult spelling words on the board. You may also choose to write "key" words and phrases on the board to aid the students' memories in recalling the order of the main points. Finally, direct the students to write the dictocomp, adhering as closely as possible to the original.

Do not expect students to write a dictocomp verbatim (as they would a dictation). Any correct version is acceptable. Grade students' work based on inclusion of important points as well as on correctness of grammar, punctuation, and spelling. Scoring should also take into account any attempt to use new rhetorical or structural items taught in the chapter.

Prewriting Activities.

A great deal of attention is given to prewriting activities. You will need to remind students again and again that writing is a continuing process, that no piece of writing is ever really finished. Reluctant writers resist being required to outline their ideas and then to write several drafts before producing the final, "polished" composition. Make every effort to insure that students do the prewriting and postwriting activities with care and thought. These exercises *will* improve students' writing!

Class Activity.

Since many students experience writer's block when trying to get started with an essay assignment, it would be very helpful for them to do a practice brainstorming session, either as a class or in small groups, on a related topic before each essay assignment at the end of each chapter.

Follow this procedure:

1. Choose a topic related to the lesson chapter.
2. Write the practice thesis statement on the board.
3. Elicit ideas from the students that would support the thesis.
4. After completing the brainstorming session, have students pick out the most important main ideas and mark them with capital letters A, B, C, etc.
5. Then, have the students pick out the lesser points that support each of the main ideas and mark them with numbers 1, 2, 3, etc.
6. Make a rough outline from the items in steps 4 and 5.

This class or group exercise will give the students the confidence they need to get started on their own essay.

Freewriting. The short freewriting assignments may or may not be graded, as you wish. If you do not grade the compositions, you might use them as "trial runs"—a means for students to try out newly acquired skills without penalty. Although topics are suggested, we encourage you and your students to develop your own topics.

Grammar. Grammar exercises may be worked through in class, assigned to individual students for remedial or supplemental work, or omitted altogether.

Sentence Structure. The sentence structure sections in Chapters 1–5 are basic and should not be omitted in most instances. However, you may choose to omit the complex sentence work in Chapters 7–10 (adjective clauses, noun clauses, adverb clauses of contrast).

On Your Own. We have suggested a variety of topics for student compositions at the end of each chapter and have marked the more challenging assignments with a star. However, we urge you to explore other topics of interest with your class that may be more relevant to their particular country, culture, or current events. Take care that topics suit the rhetorical mode of the chapter, however.

Correcting Compositions. Your task of correcting and commenting on students' drafts and final compositions is all-important. We would like to pass on a method that will lighten your load and provide maximum opportunity for the student to learn to self-correct.

If you and your students have access to cassette tape players, ask each student to give you a blank tape at the beginning of the term. Discuss each assignment with the student on the tape, pointing out errors and suggesting improvements. Hand back the tape with the assignment to the student for correction. The student revises his or her work and hands in the tape with the revised copy. Thus, you can use the tape again and again.

The advantages of using a cassette tape to correct compositions are many: The student receives more "personal" attention, and you are relieved of the necessity of *writing* copious commentary on each point needing revision (and thus spared writer's cramp with each set of papers). By merely suggesting, rather than writing in corrections, you can encourage students to think about, assess, and eventually edit their own work. For example, early in the term, you might give a lengthy explanation such as this: "You need a transition expression at the beginning of your third paragraph. Because the idea you discuss in this paragraph is additional to the main idea in your second paragraph, you need to use a transition such as 'furthermore,' 'moreover,' 'in addition,' or 'secondly.' Put the transition expression at the beginning of the paragraph, and don't forget to put a comma after it." Later in the term, a shorter hint should suffice: "You need to introduce paragraph 3 with a transition signal indicating that it discusses an additional idea."

Acknowledgments

We wish to thank our "support group"—those individuals who critiqued, always encouraged, and in many instances inspired us during the writing of this book: Eileen Hansen, Middlesex County College; Thomas H. Kitchens, University of Texas at Austin; Catherine Sadow, Northeastern University; Cathy Day, Eastern Michigan University; Elizabeth Minicz, Triton College; and Susan Vik, Boston University.

We gratefully acknowledge Cynthia Weber of the Berkeley Adult School, who field-tested the manuscript and offered excellent suggestions to improve its contents.

Finally, we wish to thank our families: Andrew Hogue, a son who had to compete with the book for attention; also, George Oshima, Suzanne, Kathleen, and, of course, Ryan. Their constant support and understanding helped to make this book become a reality.

Alice Oshima
Ann Hogue

PART I

Narrative and Descriptive Writing

1

Introductions

Model: Introducing Princess Diana

If Princess Diana were to write a composition introducing herself, it might go something like this:

1   Hello! My name is Princess Diana of Wales. I am a member of the British Royal family.

I was born on July 1, 1961, at Park House on the royal estate of Sandringham in Norfolk, England. I attended various boarding schools during my early years. My
5 favorite subject was English history. At school I studied ballet and tap dancing, and I also won swimming contests. When I was sixteen, I went to school in Switzerland. I studied French and learned to ski. After I finished school, I lived in London with three of my girlfriends, and I became a teacher at the Young England Kindergarten.

Then, my life changed completely on July 29, 1981, when I married Prince
10 Charles in St. Paul's Cathedral. On our honeymoon, we cruised the Mediterranean Sea on the royal yacht *Britannia*. After our honeymoon, I began my life as the wife of the future king of England. I visited schools and hospitals, traveled with my husband, and attended many official ceremonies. In 1982, our son William was born, and in 1984, our son Harry was born. I continued my royal duties, but I also
15 became actively involved in my children's upbringing*.

In 1992, Prince Charles and I separated. However, I still perform many royal duties, such as making an official visit to Kathmandu, meeting with the president of France, and giving a speech for European Drug Prevention Week in London. In my new life as an independent, modern career woman, I am continuing my public work
20 with AIDS patients, underprivileged* children, and the homeless. I am very concerned about world social issues.

My main interest is to bring up both of my sons to become happy, well-adjusted young men. Also, my duty is to prepare my older son, William, to become the king of England some day. My life as a princess and mother is very busy, but it is very
25 rewarding, indeed.

---

upbringing: childraising   **underprivileged:** poor

3

Questions on the Model

1. Who is Princess Diana?
2. In which paragraph do you learn this?
3. What does the second paragraph tell you about her?
4. What do you learn about Princess Diana in the third paragraph?
5. When did Prince Charles and Princess Diana separate?
6. What are some of her activities since then?
7. What is her main interest?
8. How has Princess Diana shown her independence?

ORGANIZATION

A **paragraph** is a group of related statements that a writer develops about a subject. Each paragraph is a separate unit marked by indenting the first word from the left-hand margin, or by leaving extra space above and below the paragraph.

A **composition** is a piece of writing that has more than one paragraph. It is divided into three parts: a beginning, a middle, and an end. The beginning is called the **introduction**, the middle is called the **body**, and the end is called the **conclusion**. The introduction and the conclusion are usually one paragraph each. The body may have one, two, or more paragraphs.

For example, the composition about Princess Diana that you just read has five paragraphs. The first paragraph, which introduces the topic of the composition (Princess Diana), is the introduction. The last paragraph is the conclusion. The three paragraphs in the middle are the body.

Each paragraph in the body discusses a different subject. Paragraph 2 (the first body paragraph) tells about Princess Diana's life before her marriage. Paragraph 3 (the second body paragraph) tells about her life during her marriage. Paragraph 4 (the third body paragraph) tells about her life after her separation from Prince Charles. How can you tell what the main topic of each paragraph is? The first sentence usually (but not always) tells you.

GRAMMAR AND MECHANICS

Capitalization

In English there are many rules for using capital letters. You probably know many of them already. To test your knowledge, look at the composition about Princess Diana again and write the words with capital letters in the spaces that follow. Add the rules (if you know them) in the spaces to the right.

1. <u>Hello!</u> first word in sentence
2. <u>I</u> personal pronoun in first person is always capital letters.
3. <u>My</u>
4. <u>Then</u> first word in sentence.   After
5. <u>July 1</u> Month or name always capital letters. However.
6. <u>At</u>
7. <u>Also</u>

(Continue on a separate sheet of paper.)

You may not have been able to give all the rules, but aren't you surprised at how many you already know!

CAPITALIZATION RULES

Here are some important rules for capitalization:

■ Capitalize the first word of a sentence.
> Hello! My name is Princess Diana.
> At school I studied ballet.

■ Capitalize the pronoun *I*.
> My children and I enjoy skiing.

■ Capitalize all proper nouns. Proper nouns include: *a person, place or thing*
■ Names of deities:
> God
> Allah
> Shiva

■ Names of people and their titles:
> John P. Doe
> Princess Diana of Wales
> Dr. Jonas Salk
> Professor Henry Higgins
> Mr. and Mrs. John O. Smith

(BUT: Do **not** capitalize a title without a name: the general, the prime minister, the math professor, the prince, the king.)

■ Names of specific places (places you could find on a map):
> Gary, Indiana   Lake Victoria
> Mediterranean Sea   Telegraph Avenue
> North Pole   Trafalgar Square
> Park Avenue

- Names of days, months, and special days:

Monday	Independence Day
January	Ramadan

  (BUT: Do **not** capitalize the names of the seasons.)

- Names of specific groups of people (nationalities, races, and ethnic groups), languages, and religions:

Asian	Sino-Soviet
Caucasian	Moslem
American	English
Jehovah's Witness	Arabic

- Names of geographic areas:

  the Middle East
  the North
  the Southwest

  Jane's home is in the South, but Tom comes from the East Coast.

  (BUT: Do **not** capitalize the names of compass directions: Drive east for two blocks, and then turn south.)

- Names of school subjects with course numbers:

  Chemistry 10A
  Business Administration 17B
  German 01

  (BUT: Do **not** capitalize names of classes without numbers, except languages: computer science, business administration, economics, German conversation, English composition.)

- Names of specific structures such as buildings and bridges:

  Golden Gate Bridge
  Park Plaza Hotel
  the White House
  Kensington Palace

- Names of specific organizations (businesses, clubs, schools):

  Young England Kindergarten
  Sears, Roebuck & Co.
  Sumitomo Bank
  International Students' Club
  University of California
  St. Mary's High School

- Titles of compositions, stories, books, magazines, newspapers, plays, poems, and movies:

  Introducing Myself
  Introduction to Academic Writing
  Star Wars
  All Quiet on the Western Front

NOTE: Capitalize the first word, the last word, and other important words in titles. Do **not** capitalize short words such as articles (*a, an, the*), prepositions (*of, on, for*), and conjunctions (*and, but, or*). Of course, you *must* capitalize a short word if it is the first word in a title.

A Tale of Two Cities

Also, underline the titles of books, magazines, newspapers, and movies.

PRACTICE: Capitalization

A. Change the small letters to capital letters wherever it is necessary in the following sentences.

1. farnaz is a student from iran. she speaks english, french, and farsi. her major is chemistry.

2. the three most important holidays in the united states are christmas, thanksgiving, and easter.

3. president john f. kennedy was born on may 29, 1917, and was assassinated* on november 22, 1963.

4. green hills college is located in boston, massachusetts.

5. i am taking four classes this semester: english 40, sociology 32, typing, and a computer science course.

6. thanksgiving is always on the third thursday in november.

7. excuse me! can you please tell me where the golden gate bridge is?

8. there are three main religions in japan: buddhism, shintoism, and christianity.

9. in the united states, there is no school during the months of june, july, and august. this is the summer vacation.

10. i read a good book last weekend called *the old man and the sea* by ernest hemingway.

B. Answer the following questions with complete sentences. Capitalize correctly.

1. What is your full name? (first, middle, family name)

_____

_____

---

assassinated: murdered

2. Where are you from? (city and country)

_____

3. What languages do you speak?

_____

4. What important holidays do you have in your country?

_____

5. What is the name of your school or college?

_____

6. What are your favorite school subjects?

_____

C. Copy the following letter to Kazumi from her friend Tomiko and change small letters to capital letters wherever it is necessary. Notice that the salutation (greeting) *Dear* and the closing word *Love* are both capitalized.

1

san francisco, ca 94127
october 12, 1992

Dear kazumi,

1   well, here i am in san francisco. i can hardly believe it. san francisco
5 is a beautiful city. it has many interesting places to visit. i like it here very much.

2   let me tell you about san francisco. it looks just like the pictures in travel
books! yesterday i took a bus tour around the city and saw many famous
places: golden gate park, the golden gate bridge, chinatown, and
fisherman's wharf. on saturday i took a boat trip to famous alcatraz island in
10 the middle of san francisco bay. i am staying at the hyatt regency hotel, which
is one of the newest hotels in the city.

3   today is a special day in the united states, especially in san francisco. it is
october 12, which is columbus day. on columbus day, americans celebrate the
discovery of the new world on october 12, 1492 by christopher columbus, who
15 was italian. there are many italian-american people in san francisco, and they
always have a big celebration on columbus day here.

4   right now i am sitting in union square, which is a small park in the middle
of the main shopping district. it is a warm and sunny day. there are many
people in the square. some of them are sitting on the grass eating lunch, some
20 of them are reading, and some of them are sleeping.

5   tomorrow i will fly to los angeles, which is south of san francisco. there i
will visit hollywood and disneyland. after that, i will fly home on japan air
lines. i will arrive on saturday, october 31. i hope you can meet me at the
airport. i can't wait to see you!

25   Love,

                                                        Tomiko

PRACTICE: Paragraphing

Write down the main topic of each body paragraph (paragraphs 2, 3,
and 4) in Tomiko's letter.

1. Introduction

2. _Places about San Francisco_

3. _Today (October 12) is_ an especially day.

4. _The small park that I_ in now.

5. Conclusion

Punctuation

Punctuation is necessary to make sentence meaning clear. The meanings of these two sentences are different:

> Stop Bill.
> Stop, Bill.

The first sentence tells someone to stop Bill. The second sentence tells Bill to stop.

END-OF-SENTENCE PUNCTUATION RULES

There are three punctuation marks that you can use at the end of a sentence: the period, the question mark, and the exclamation mark.

- Put a period (full stop) at the end of a statement.

  My name is Jennifer Wong.
  I don't like to give interviews.

- Put a question mark at the end of a question.

  What is your name?
  Do you speak English?

- Put an exclamation mark at the end of a sentence to show strong feeling.

  It sure is hot today!
  I am just crazy about soccer!

  CAUTION: Do not overuse exclamation marks. To understand why you should not, compare these two paragraphs:

  > The telephone rang at midnight! I ran to answer it! I didn't hear a voice! I said, "Hello! Hello!" There was no answer! I was frightened!

  > The telephone rang at midnight. I ran to answer it. I didn't hear a voice. I said, "Hello? Hello?" There was no answer. I was frightened!

The first paragraph has too many exclamation marks. The second paragraph, with only one exclamation mark at the end of the last sentence to show strong feeling, is more effective.

DICTOCOMP

When your instructor dictates this paragraph to you, be sure to use correct punctuation and capitalization as you write it down.

1   Hello! My name is Roberto Sanchez. I was born on September 21, 1975, in the large city of San Juan, Puerto Rico. I am a student at Green Hills College in Boston, Massachusetts. I am studying English now, but I want to study business or economics later. I am from Puerto Rico, so my native language is Spanish. There are nine
5 people in my family. I have four brothers and two sisters. My favorite pastime is playing video games, and my favorite sport is soccer. I like studying in the United States, but I miss my family very much.

FREEWRITING

Using the dictocomp as a model, write a paragraph about yourself. Include interesting information about yourself, your activities, and your family. Start with:

Hello! My name is _____.

SENTENCE STRUCTURE

Simple Sentences/Parts of a Sentence

A **sentence** is a group of words that contains at least one subject and one verb. A sentence expresses a complete thought. There are four kinds of sentences in English: *simple* sentences, *compound* sentences, *complex* sentences, and *compound-complex* sentences. First, we will learn about simple sentences.

A **simple sentence** has one subject and one verb. The **subject** tells *who* or *what* did something. The **verb** tells the *action* (or condition).

These are simple sentences:

Subject	Verb
I	study.
I	study and work.
My head	hurts.
My head and neck	hurt.
It	is raining.
The students	are reading.

(Notice that the subject in a simple sentence may be compound: *My head and neck* hurt. Also, the verb in a simple sentence may be compound: I *study and work.*)

NOTE: "Save your money" is also a complete sentence. The subject "you" is understood and not included.

A sentence may also have a complement (but it does not *have* to have one). The **complement** completes the meaning of the verb or adds more information to the sentence. There are many types of complements. A complement in a simple sentence may be a noun, pronoun, adjective, or adverb.

Subject	Verb	Complement
I	study	English. (noun)
I	don't understand	you. (pronoun)
His girlfriend	is	pretty. (adjective)
It	isn't raining	now. (adverb)

A complement may also be a noun phrase, a verb phrase, or a prepositional phrase.

My father	owns	his own business. (noun phrase)
My girlfriend	wants	to get married. (verb phrase)
The students	are reading	in the library. (prepositional phrase)

A complement may also be a combination.

I	study	English at Rolling Hills College. (noun + prepositional phrase)
She	wants	to get married soon. (verb phrase + adverb)

Subject-Verb Agreement

You already know that subjects and verbs must agree in number. You should write:

> My sister is married. (singular)
> My sisters are married. (plural)
> My brother and my sister are single. (plural)

Sometimes students make mistakes in subject-verb agreement when the subject has a prepositional phrase following it. For this reason, you should learn to recognize prepositional phrases.

A **prepositional phrase** is a group of words that begins with a preposition and ends with a noun. A prepositional phrase usually tells where, when, how, or why.

from Mexico City	in the morning
on December 25	of my sisters
to my best friend	around the room
by bus	because of the weather

A prepositional phrase may come after the subject of a sentence, but *it is not part of the subject.* Therefore, you should ignore* it most of the time when you are trying to decide which verb form to use.

> One (of my sisters) is also a singer.

(The subject is *one,* which is singular.)

Here are some other examples:

Singular subjects:
One of my brothers is a musician.
Neither of my parents is living.
Much of my time is spent in the library.
Each of my brothers wants his own car.
Either of my sisters can babysit for you tonight.

Plural subjects:
Both of my parents are teachers.
Several of the teachers speak my language.

But sometimes telling a singular subject from a plural subject isn't that easy, unfortunately. A few words can be either singular or plural. In these cases, you must refer to the noun in the prepositional phrase.

> Some of the money was missing. (singular)
> Some of the students were missing. (plural)
> All of my time is spent in the library. (singular)
> All of my brothers are singers. (plural)
> Most of the ice was melted. (singular)
> Most of the ice cubes were melted. (plural)
> A lot of the work was too easy. (singular)
> A lot of the people were angry. (plural)

---

ignore: pay no attention to

PRACTICE: Identifying Subjects, Verbs, and Complements

Underline the subjects, verbs, and complements in the following sentences and write S, V, or C above them. Also, put parentheses ( ) around prepositional phrases.

1. My name is Roberto Sanchez.

2. I was born (on September 21, 1966)(in the city)(of San Juan, Puerto Rico.)

3. My oldest sister is married and has two children.

4. I am a student (at Green Hills College)(in Boston, Massachusetts.)

5. Boston is the capital (of Massachusetts.)

6. Some (of my classes) are difficult.

7. Some (of the homework) is boring.

8. Most (of my classmates) are friendly.

9. None (of my classmates) speaks Spanish.

10. A lot (of my classes) are (in Dante Hall.)

11. A lot (of my time) is spent (in the student lounge.)

12. I am (from Puerto Rico.)

13. My native language is Spanish.

14. My father works (in an office.)

15. I have four brothers and two sisters.

16. None (of us) is married.

17. All (of us) are single.

18. My youngest brother and sister are (still in high school.)

19. My oldest brother studies (in the morning) and works (in the afternoon.)

20. In the evening I watch television or play cards.

21. My father understands English (but doesn't speak it.)

22. (In my country) most (of the people) are Catholics.

23. Neither (of my parents) has been (in the United States.)

PRACTICE: Simple Sentences

A. Rewrite each sentence to make the subject (compound.) Don't forget to make the verb plural!

1. Akiko is studying electrical engineering.

Akiko and Roberto are studying electrical engineering.

2. My brother lives in an apartment in Paris.

My brother and sister live in an apartment in Paris.

3. My mother speaks six languages.

My mother and father speak six languages.

4. English is my favorite subject. (CAREFUL! What other word—besides the verb—do you have to make plural?)

English and German are my favorite subjects.

B. In these sentences, make the subject singular. Don't forget to make the verb agree with the subject!

1. My girlfriend and I want to get married next summer.

My girlfriend wants to get married next summer.

or

I want to get married next summer.

2. My oldest brother and my youngest sister are married.

My oldest brother is married.

3. My mother and father live in Rome.

My father lives in Rome.

4. My friends and I eat lunch in the student cafeteria.

I eat lunch in the student cafeteria.

C. Rewrite each incomplete sentence and add the missing element: subject, verb, or complement.

1. My roommate's name Alex.

My roommate's name is Alex.

2. Is from the East Coast

*He is from the East Coast.***or** *Is he from the East Coast?*

3. Alex's family lives

Alex's family lives in Boston.

4. Alex and I in the dorm

Alex and I are in the dorm.

5. Our room very small

Our room is very small.

6. Our schedules different

Our schedules are different.

7. I like to sleep late, but Alex gets up

I like to sleep late, but Alex (likes to) gets up early. *likes to gets lat*

8. Tries not to wake me up

She tries not to wake me up

9. Is a very considerate roommate

Is he a very considerate roommate?

10. He is

He is a good man.

11. In the afternoon we

In the afternoon, we went to cafeteria to eat lunch.

12. Alex speaks

Alex speaks Chinese.

13. Alex me with my homework

Alex tells me with my homework. *helps*

14. We often go

We often goes to supermaket to buy some food.

ON YOUR OWN! (Student Composition)

A. Choose one of the following topics and write a paragraph.

> Your favorite friend or family member
> A class or teacher you hated
> Your favorite or least favorite city

Your first sentence should state what you are going to write about.

> ### Example:
>
> My sixth grade teacher, Mr. Lemon, was always mean to all the students.
>
> (Now write a few sentences to explain how he was a mean teacher. Give an example about a time he was mean to you. To end your paragraph, write your final personal statement about the teacher you hated.)

★ **B.** Write a composition about one of your classmates that is like the model at the beginning of the chapter.

First, interview him or her to find out some facts. Find out his or her full name, date and place of birth, major subject, future career, what languages he or she speaks, or any other basic facts. Write this information in your first paragraph.

Write about your classmate's family in your second paragraph. Is he or she married? How many brothers and sisters or children does he or she have?

In your third paragraph, tell about his or her special hobbies or interests.

Write a short (one or two sentences) final comment about your classmate in the fourth (concluding) paragraph.

An outline of your composition might look like this:

> I. Introduction (facts about your classmate)
> II. My classmate's family
> III. Hobbies, interests, or special talents
> IV. Conclusion (your personal remarks about your classmate)

Hints for Success

- Vary your sentence openings. Do not always use the subject-verb-complement pattern. Begin some of your sentences with prepositional phrases.
- Check your composition carefully for correct spelling, capitalization, and punctuation before you hand it in.

chapter 2

Narration

Model: A Traditional American Wedding

1   June 17, 1993

Dear Charo,

Last weekend, I had the most wonderful experience! I attended the wedding of
two of my friends from college. The bride* was Jennifer Mason, and the groom*
5 was Scott Dixon. They became engaged last year, but they wanted to wait until
they had both graduated from college before getting married. Anyway, I thought
you would like to hear about a traditional* American wedding and what happens
on the wedding day.

First, the guests arrive at the church. The ushers* meet them at the door and
10 help them find seats. Friends and family of the bride always sit on the left side of the
church, and friends and family of the groom always sit on the right. The parents of
the couple always sit in the front.

Next, the groom and his best man* enter the church and stand in front. Then, a
musician begins to play the "Wedding March," and the bridesmaids* begin to
15 march slowly down the aisle* from the back toward the front of the church. Finally,
the bride appears and walks down the aisle beside her father. The bride usually
wears a white wedding dress and veil, and she always carries a bouquet of flowers
in her hands.

Now, everyone is at the front of the church, so the marriage ceremony can
20 begin. During the ceremony, the groom always gives the bride a wedding ring, and
the bride sometimes gives the groom one, too. At last, the religious official says,

---

bride: woman who is getting married   **best man:** man who helps the groom
groom: man who is getting married   **bridesmaid:** woman who helps the bride
traditional: refers to a custom or practice   **aisle:** path between rows of seats
   handed down from the past
usher: person who helps guests find their seats at a church or theater

"I now pronounce you husband and wife,"* and the couple is now married. The bride and groom kiss and then leave the church arm in arm. The guests throw rice over the couple outside the church as they leave.

25   The last big event is the wedding reception. This is a big party after the ceremony. Everyone brings or sends a gift, so the young couple often doesn't need to buy a lot of things for their house or apartment. The wedding reception may be a dinner, or it may be an afternoon party with only snacks*. Champagne is usually served, and everyone eats, drinks, and dances for many hours. The bride throws her

30 flowers to the unmarried girls before she and her husband leave the reception. According to tradition, the girl who catches the flowers will be the next one to get married.

    I hope you have enjoyed my story about a traditional American wedding. Of course, not everyone in the U.S. has a big wedding like this one. It is very expensive,

35 and not everyone can afford it.

    Write soon. I am eager to hear about your vacation.

Love,

Anna

Questions on the Model

1. What does Anna write to her friend Charo about?
2. What does the first paragraph tell about? When was Jennifer and Scott's wedding? What tense does Anna use to write about it, present or past?
3. What do paragraphs 2, 3, 4, and 5 tell about? What tense does Anna use for them?

ORGANIZATION

Narration: Time Order

    The letter from Anna to her friend Charo that you just read tells about the events in a traditional American wedding. Anna writes about the events in the order in which they happen. This is called **chronological** or **time order.**

    The first paragraph is the **introduction.** It introduces the topic of the letter in general: American weddings. The last paragraph is the **conclusion.** It ends the letter with general statements and gives Anna's final comment.

    The four paragraphs in the middle are the **body.** Notice that each paragraph of the body tells about specific* events that take place in one particular time block. For example, the three paragraphs that begin with the words *First, Next,* and *Now* discuss three separate stages in the marriage ceremony: (1) the arrival of the guests, (2) the march down the aisle by the bridesmaids and the bride, and (3) the ceremony itself. The next paragraph explains an event that happens still later—after the ceremony.

"I now pronounce you husband and wife": I say officially that you are now married.
snack: something eaten between meals   **specific:** certain

An outline of the letter would look like this:

      I. Introduction
     II. Body
         A. Arrival of the guests
         B. March down the aisle
         C. The ceremony
         D. The reception
    III. Conclusion

Time Order Words and Phrases

Notice the kinds of words and phrases used to show time order. These are called time order words or phrases because they show the order in which events happen.

Words	Phrases
first (second, etc.)	before the wedding
then	on Saturday
next	until midnight
finally	after that
afterward	in the morning
meanwhile	in the meantime

at the same time.

Time order words and phrases are followed by a comma if they come at the beginning of a sentence.

PRACTICE: Chronological Order

A. Turn back to Anna's letter on pages 19–20. Draw a circle around all of the time order words and phrases you find. Notice that almost every paragraph begins with a time order expression, and some paragraphs have time order expressions within them.

B. The following sets of sentences are not in correct time order. Number the sentences in the correct order.

1. _7_ She put the clean dishes away.

   _2_ She removed the dirty dishes from the table.

   _5_ She turned on the dishwasher.

   _4_ She put them in the dishwasher.

   _3_ She piled* them in the sink and rinsed* them.

   _1_ It was Sarah's turn to wash the dishes last night.

   _6_ Finally, the dishes were clean.

---

piled: put several things on top of each other   **rinsed:** washed in clean water

reference
dictionary
atlas
encyclopedia
almanac (every year)

2. _7_ He filled it out and left.

_4_ He went to the bookshelf, but the book wasn't there.

_1_ Tom went to the library.

_2_ He went to the card catalog.

_6_ The librarian told him to fill out a reserve slip.*

_5_ He told the librarian he wanted to reserve that book.

_3_ He wrote down the title and call number* of the book.

3. _3_ They chose a dining table and six chairs.

_1_ Mr. and Mrs. Smith went shopping today.

_5_ He gave it to the salesperson.

_2_ They took the escalator* down to the furniture department.

_4_ Mr. Smith took his credit card out of his wallet.

_6_ The salesperson wrote up a bill of sale.

4. _4_ Check the inside of the victim's mouth for anything that would prevent free breathing.

_5_ Cover the victim's mouth completely with your mouth and pinch* his or her nose shut with one hand.

_3_ Push the victim's head back so that his or her chin is pointing up.

_1_ To give mouth-to-mouth resuscitation* effectively*, follow these steps:

_6_ Blow four quick, full breaths of air into his or her mouth.

_7_ Remove your mouth and wait for the air to flow out.

_2_ Lay the victim flat on his or her back, face up.

_8_ Repeat this procedure ten to twelve times a minute until the victim begins to breathe on his or her own or until help arrives.

---

reserve slip: piece of paper used to reserve a library book
call number: identifying number of a library book
escalator: moving stair
pinch: press tightly between the thumb and finger
resuscitation: act of bringing back to life   **effectively:** achieving the intended purpose

C. Write the sentences from the preceding exercise as single paragraphs. Try to make your paragraphs flow smoothly by using these three techniques: (1) Add time order words or phrases at the beginning of some of the sentences to show chronological order. (2) Combine some of the sentences to form simple sentences with compound verbs. (3) Change nouns to pronouns where possible.

Example:

It was Sarah's turn to wash the dishes last night. First, she removed the dirty dishes from the table. Next, she piled them in the sink and rinsed them. After that, she put them in the dishwasher and turned it on. Finally, the dishes were clean, so she put them away.

GRAMMAR AND MECHANICS

Simple Present Tense

The **simple present tense** is the verb tense used to state facts and describe repeated activities. In her letter, Anna uses the simple past tense in the first paragraph to write about the wedding of her friends on a weekend in the past. This was a specific event at a specific time in the past. However, in the remainder* of the letter, she writes about traditional American weddings in general—not a specific one. She writes about the events that traditionally happen again and again. Therefore, she uses the simple present tense.

PRACTICE: Simple Present Tense

Answer the following questions about Anna's letter. Write complete sentences.

1. Who meets the guests at the door of the church?

The ushers meet them.

2. What is the ushers' job?

Person who helps guests find their seats at a church or theater.

3. Where do friends of the couple sit in the church?

The friends of the groom sit on the right. always on the left.

4. Where do the parents of the couple sit?

The parents of the couple always sit in the front

---

remainder: something left over

5. Where do the groom and the best man stand and wait?

The groom and the best man stand in front

6. What does the bride's father do?

The bride appears and walks down the aisle beside her father.

7. What does the bride usually wear?

The bride usually wears a white wedding dress and veil.

8. Does she carry anything in her hands?

Yes, she always carries a bouquet of flowers in her hands.

9. Do the bride and groom give each other wedding rings? _The groom always give —_

Yes, the bride and groom give each other wedding rings.

10. What happens as the couple leaves the church?

The bride and groom kiss an then. —

11. What do the guests bring to the wedding reception?

Everyone brings or sends a gift.

Adverbs of Frequency

Adverbs of frequency are words like _always, usually, sometimes,_ and _often._ These words tell how often something happens.

RULES FOR USING ADVERBS OF FREQUENCY

Place an adverb of frequency:

- Before the main verb:
  Women often cry at weddings.
- After all helping verbs in positive sentences. The helping verbs are _am, are, is, was, were, have, has, had, do, does, did, shall, should, can, could, will, would, may, might, must._
  The maid of honor* is usually the bride's sister or best friend.
  The bride doesn't always give the groom a wedding ring.

  NOTE: If the helping verb is negative—_isn't, doesn't, won't,_ and so on—the adverbs _sometimes, frequently,_ and _occasionally_ come before it. _Usually, often,_ and _generally_ can come before or after it. _Sometimes_ may also come at the beginning of a sentence.

---

maid of honor: most important bridesmaid

Here are some additional examples of the use of adverbs of frequency, showing their meanings:

100 percent of the time:	A wedding guest should <u>always</u> bring or send a gift.
80 percent of the time:	The bride <u>usually</u> wears a white wedding dress and veil.
60 percent of the time:	Couples <u>often</u> get married in a church.
40 percent of the time:	The bride <u>sometimes</u> gives the groom a ring.
20 percent of the time:	In the United States, parents <u>seldom</u> choose their children's marriage partners for them.
10 percent of the time:	A wife is <u>rarely</u> older than her husband.
0 percent of the time:	A bride <u>never</u> wears a red wedding dress.

PRACTICE: Simple Present Tense and Adverbs of Frequency

A. Fill in the blanks in the following paragraph with the correct adverb of frequency and the correct form of the verb given in parentheses before each blank. To express frequency, choose from *sometimes, always, never, usually, often,* and *seldom.*

Example:
Mr. Wright (all of the time/work) *always works* from 6:30 A.M. to 7:00 P.M., six days a week.

1   Mr. and Mrs. Wright are an elderly couple. Mr. Wright owns a corner

grocery store. Mrs. Wright is a housewife. Mr. Wright works hard every day,

so at the end of the day, he comes home very tired. He (every evening/

like) _always   like_____ to watch television in the

5 evenings. He (not at all/want) _____never   wants_____

to go out at night, so Mrs. Wright (once in a while/complain)

_sometimes   complains_____ to him. She (most of the time/

like) _____usually   likes_____ to go out to dinner or

visit with friends. After all, she (most of the time/watch)

10 _____usually   watches_____ soap operas* during the day,

so in the evenings, she (not often/enjoy) _____seledom   enjoys_____

staying home. This causes a family problem, and the Wrights (now and then/

spend) _____sometimes   spend_____ the evening arguing. Then,

they are both unhappy.

B. Write sentences by answering the following yes/no questions. Use an adverb of frequency in each sentence: *usually, often, sometimes, seldom, always,* and *never.*

1. Do you gamble?*

_Yes, I sometimes gamble at cards._____

2. Are you lucky?

_No, I often win by playing well._____

3. Do you go to American movies?

_Yes, I seldom go to American movies._____

4. Are American movies boring?

_No, American are seledom boring._____

5. Do you have time for fun?

_No, I seledom have time to fun._____

---

soap opera: continuing television story about the lives and problems of the same people
gamble: play games of chance for money

6. Do you go out on dates*?

Yes, I sometimes go out on dates.

7. Do you go to discos?

Yes, I rarely go to discos.

8. Do you eat fast foods*?

Yes, I sometimes eat fast foods.

9. Do you eat at McDonald's?

Yes, I seldom eat at McDonald's.

10. Do you watch television?

Yes, I often watch television.

11. Do you play sports?

Yes, I sometimes go swimming.

12. Are you a "good sport"* when you lose a game?

Yes, I am sometimes a "good sport"

COMMA RULES

Commas are used within a sentence in the following ways:

■ To separate words, phrases, or clauses in a series (a group of three or more):

> Everyone eats, drinks, dances, and has a good time at a wedding.
> Members of the wedding include the bride, groom, best man, maid of honor, ushers, and bridesmaids.

NOTE: Do **not** use a comma if there are only two items.

> The bride enters the church and walks down the aisle.

■ To separate the parts of dates and addresses, **except** before ZIP codes:

> The Smith family lives at 3237 Atlantic Avenue, Pittsburgh, Pennsylvania 66711. They moved there on January 1, 1990.

---

go out on dates: go out in the evening with a person of the opposite sex
fast food: food that is prepared and eaten quickly, such as hamburgers or pizza
good sport: someone who can lose with a smile

- After time order expressions:

    First, the guests arrive at the church.
    Next, the groom and the best man appear.
    Then, the music begins.
    After that, the bridesmaids walk down the aisle.
    Finally, the bride appears.
    After the ceremony, there is a big party.

- Before the coordinating conjunction in a compound sentence (that is, to separate the first simple sentence from the second simple sentence when the two are joined together by one of these words: *and, but, so, or, nor, for, yet*):

    The bride was Jennifer Mason, and the groom was Scott Dixon.
    The best man is usually the groom's brother, but he may also be a close friend.
    The wedding reception may be a dinner, or it may be an afternoon party.

[handwritten margin note: for, and, nor, but, or, yet, so — Co-ordinating conjunctions]

NOTE: **Never** start a line with a comma, period, question mark, or exclamation mark.

WRONG: George and I left the party at twelve o'clock , and the Smiths left with us.

RIGHT: George and I left the party at twelve o'clock, and the Smiths left with us.

PRACTICE: Punctuation

A. Add commas, periods, question marks, and/or exclamation marks wherever they are necessary in the following sentences.

1. Daisy, Tomiko, Keiko, and Nina share an apartment near the school.

2. The address of their apartment is 3245 North Lafayette Street, Chicago, Illinois 80867.

3. Tomiko and Keiko are from Japan, and Nina and Daisy are from Venezuela.

4. Nina and Keiko have the same birthday. Both of the girls were born on June 3, 1968.

5. How old are they today?

6. All of the girls like to cook, but none of them likes to wash the dishes afterward.

7. That is typical!

8. They have delicious meals. Last night, they ate Japanese tempura, Venezuelan *arroz con pollo*, Chinese vegetables, and American ice cream.

9. First, Nina made the rice. Then, Keiko cooked the tempura. After that, Tomiko prepared the vegetables.

10. After dinner, Daisy served the dessert.

11. They could choose chocolate or vanilla ice cream, or they could have vanilla ice cream with chocolate sauce.

46 1946.
35 1971
4 21. 1973

B. Answer the following questions with complete sentences.

1. Where were you born?

I was born in San Juan, Puerto Rico.

2. When were you born? (Begin your answer with: "I was born on . . .")

I was born on July 13, 1973.

3. What is your address in this country?

My address is 1983 N. Palm Canyon Dr, Palm Springs, CA 92262.

4. What is today's date?

It is June 8, 1994.

5. What are three of your favorite foods?

(Three of) My favorite foods are vegetables salad, see foods, and Chinese foods.

6. What do you usually do on weekends? (Name at least four activities.)

On weekends, I usually go shopping, go swimming, and enjoy my favorite food.

7. What <u>elementary</u> school did you attend, and where did (do) you go to high school? *home. economic I attend from ○ kindgardan. Tainan junior college. Tainan. I went to ○ in Tainan.*

8. What are two or three goals in your life?

I am going to be a good teacher. peacefully
I am I want to be a sussesful woman.

C. In the following paragraphs, change the small letters to capital letters wherever necessary. Also add punctuation (periods and commas).

1   koji matsumura lives in tokyo, japan with his family. he is a vice
president in the international banking department of the mitsui national
bank. mr. matsumura received his master's degree* in business administration from the university of hawaii in june, 1981.

5   last winter, he went on a business trip to los angeles on the west coast
and to new york city on the atlantic coast. when he was in new york, he
walked in central park, visited the united nations building, and shopped
on fifth avenue.

    he returned home in time to celebrate new year's day with his
10 family. new year's day is an important day in japan. it is on january 1 of
every year.

---

master's degree: university diploma above a BA (bachelor's degree) and below a PhD (doctor's degree)

DICTOCOMP

When your instructor dictates this paragraph to you, remember the comma rules you have learned. Draw a circle around all the time order words and phrases that you find.

Before the Wedding

1   Many parties take place before the wedding day in a traditional American wedding. First, there is sometimes an engagement party when the couple becomes engaged. Next, friends of the bride give bridal showers for her. Then, there is often a rehearsal dinner a few evenings before the wedding. All of the members of the
5   wedding go to the church to practice. Afterward, they go to a restaurant for dinner. Finally, on the night before the wedding, friends of the groom often give a bachelor party for him to celebrate his last night as an unmarried man. In conclusion, a lot of parties precede* a big American wedding!

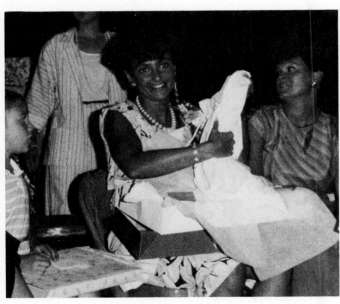

FREEWRITING

Using the three paragraphs about Koji Matsumura as a model, write two or three paragraphs about the career of your father, mother, another family member, a friend, or a relative. Describe the person's job or career and add some details about his or her activities. Start with a sentence like:

My father, Cheng Ho, lives in Taipei, Taiwan.

---

precede: to come or go before in time, place, order, or importance

SENTENCE STRUCTURE

Compound Sentences with *and, but, so, or*

A **compound sentence** is composed of two simple sentences joined together by a comma and a **coordinating conjunction.** There are seven coordinating conjunctions in English: *and, but, so, or, for, nor,* and *yet.* In this chapter, you will learn to use the first four.

RULES FOR USING COORDINATING CONJUNCTIONS

■ *and* joins sentences that are alike.

> The bride's guests sit on the left, and the groom's guests sit on the right.

■ *but* joins sentences that are opposite or show contrast.

> The bride's father pays for the wedding, but he doesn't pay for the rehearsal dinner.

■ *so* joins sentences when the second sentence expresses the result of something described in the first sentence.

> The party lasted until midnight, so everyone was tired.

■ *or* joins sentences that give choices or alternatives.

> The bride may have one bridesmaid, or she may have several.

NOTE: Use a comma before the coordinating conjunction in compound sentences only. Do not use a comma when joining compound elements in simple sentences.

Notice the difference:

> Compound sentence:
> The bride may have one bridesmaid, or she may have several.
> Simple sentence with a compound complement:
> The bride may have one bridesmaid or several.
> Compound sentence:
> They wanted to get married immediately, but they decided to wait until June.
> Simple sentence with a compound verb:
> They wanted to get married immediately but decided to wait until June.

PRACTICE: Compound Sentences with *and, but, so, or*

A. Copy all of the compound sentences from the model on pages 19-20 onto a sheet of paper. Underline the subjects once and the verbs twice.

> **Example:**
> The bride was Jennifer Mason, and the groom was Scott Dixon.

B. Decide which of the following are compound sentences and which are simple sentences. Write CS or SS in the space at the left, and add commas to the compound sentences. Underline the subjects and verbs.

_CS_ **1.** Some states allow you to get married at age fourteen, but most states require you to be sixteen.

_SS_ **2.** Couples may get married in a church or in a government office.

_SS_ **3.** A religious official or a government official may perform the marriage ceremony.

_CS_ **4.** The bride's family pays for the wedding, but the groom's family pays for the rehearsal dinner.

_SS_ **5.** The groom enters the church and waits for his bride at the front.

_SS_ **6.** The friends of the groom write "Just Married" on the young couple's car and tie old shoes, and tin cans to the rear bumper*.

_SS_ **7.** The bride usually wears a white dress and carries a bouquet of flowers in her hands.

_CS_ **8.** The bachelor party lasted until 3:00 A.M., so the groom was late to his own wedding.

C. Make compound sentences or simple sentences with compound complements by joining the following pairs of sentences with one of these coordinating conjunctions: *and, but, so, or.* Punctuate carefully.

1. After marriage, the bride may take her husband's family name, or
~~S~~ ~~s~~he may keep her own family name.

2. Today's liberated* women do not want to lose their family names, But
However, they want to add their husbands' family names. (Omit *however*.)

3. They don't want to drop their family names, So They add their husbands' family names with a hyphen—for example, Jennifer Mason-Dixon.

4. Traditionally, the bride's father pays for the wedding, He also pays for the couple's honeymoon.*

5. Many young people are financially independent. So They pay for their own wedding and honeymoon.

6. Wedding guests may bring a gift to the wedding reception, or They may send a gift to the bride's home before the wedding.

---

bumper: protective bar at the back end of a car   **liberated:** having freedom of action
honeymoon: vacation trip after a wedding

7. In this chapter, we read about a traditional wedding. Not all weddings are traditional.

[handwritten above: but]

8. Some people get married at home. Some people get married in nontraditional places such as parks.

[handwritten above: and]

D. Write compound sentences using the coordinating conjunctions you have learned. Follow the directions given.

1. Write a sentence that tells one thing you like to do and one thing you don't like to do.

> **Example:**
>
> I like to swim, but I don't like to play tennis.

2. Write a sentence about your parents. Tell something about them that is different. *[handwritten: My parents are kind person. Both they look like very young.]*

3. Write a sentence that tells two things you do every morning after you get up. *[handwritten: I washed my face and teeth. (I brush)]*

4. Write a sentence that tells two things you *might* do during your next vacation. *[handwritten: I might to go to another country and study more. (I might to)]*

5. Write a sentence that tells two things you never do. *[handwritten: I never eat mice and ski.]*

6. Write sentences that tell the results of the following. Begin each sentence with "I am/was . . ."

a. being born in (your country)

> **Example:** *[handwritten: I was born in Taiwan, so I speak Chinese.]*
>
> I was born in France, so I speak French.

b. being the oldest child/youngest child/middle child/only child in your family *[handwritten: I has a older sister and I am youngest child in my family.]*

c. being unusually tall/short/fat/thin/beautiful/handsome *[handwritten: I am short, fat and beautiful girl. I am]*

d. being a lazy/diligent student *[handwritten: I am a diligent student, but I like to sleep.]*

7. Write a sentence that tells two different careers you *might* have in the future. *[handwritten: I might to be a music, or businesswoman. (teacher)]*

E. All of the sentences in the following paragraphs are simple sentences. The paragraphs would flow much more smoothly if some of the sentences were compound or had compound verbs.

Rewrite the paragraphs, combining the sentences as described in the numbered directions on page 36. Be careful to use coordinating conjunctions that fit the meaning.

Sentences 1 through 5 are done for you.

Example:

1. Copy sentence 1 without change.
2. Combine sentences 2 and 3.
3. Combine sentences 4 and 5.

I had a terrible day today! I woke up late, so I had to hurry. I was hungry, but I didn't eat any breakfast. I got dressed, . . .

My Terrible Day

(1) I had a terrible day today! (2) I woke up late. (3) I had to hurry. (4) I was hungry. (5) I didn't eat any breakfast. (6) I got dressed. (7) I grabbed my books. (8) I ran all the way to the bus stop. (9) The bus was just pulling away. (10) I yelled. (11) The bus driver didn't hear me. (12) I could take a taxi to school. (13) I could walk. (14) I decided to walk.

(15) One hour later, I arrived at school. (16) I had missed my first class. (17) I was late to my second one. (18) After lunch, I had a chemistry test. (19) I hadn't studied for it. (20) Of course, I failed it.

(21) After school, I walked to the bus stop. (22) It started to rain. (23) I hadn't brought my umbrella. (24) I got soaked. (25) Finally, the bus came. (26) I got on. (27) I reached into my pocket for my bus fare. (28) My pocket was empty. (29) My money was gone! (30) I couldn't pay the bus fare. (31) I had to walk home in the rain.

(32) At last I got home. (33) I cooked dinner. (34) I burned everything.

(35) I ate it anyway. (36) I washed the dishes. (37) I did my homework. (38) I went to bed. (39) In the middle of the night, my bed collapsed. (40) I fell on the floor. (41) I could get up and fix my bed. (42) I could sleep on the floor. (43) I was very tired. (44) I decided to sleep on the floor the rest of the night.

(45) I certainly hope tomorrow will be a better day!

1. Copy sentence 1 without change.
2. Combine sentences 2 and 3.
3. Combine sentences 4 and 5.
4. Combine sentences 6, 7, and 8.
5. Copy sentence 9 without change.
6. Combine sentences 10 and 11.
7. Combine sentences 12 and 13.
8. Copy sentence 14 without change.

9. Copy sentence 15 without change.
10. Combine sentences 16 and 17.
11. Copy sentence 18 without change.
12. Combine sentences 19 and 20.

13. Copy sentence 21 without change.
*14. Combine sentences 22, 23, and 24.
15. Combine sentences 25 and 26.
16. Combine sentences 27 and 28.
17. Copy sentence 29 without change.
18. Combine sentences 30 and 31.

19. Copy sentence 32 without change.
*20. Combine sentences 33, 34, and 35.
21. Combine sentences 36, 37, and 38.
22. Combine sentences 39 and 40.
23. Combine sentences 41 and 42.
24. Combine sentences 43 and 44.
25. Copy sentence 45 without change.

Note: Your answers to the two starred sentences will be compound sentences with *three* independent clauses instead of two.

Example:
I don't like to cook, but my roommate does, so she does all the cooking.

ON YOUR OWN!

A. Write a paragraph in which you explain how an important holiday, birthdays, or any other important event is celebrated in your country.

Your first sentence should tell what you are writing about.

Example:

Birthdays are important in my country, so we have many special birthday customs. (Then write some sentences that tell how a typical birthday is celebrated. To end your paragraph, make a general comment about the importance of birthdays in your culture.)

★ **B.** Write a composition in which you explain an important event in your country to a friend in the United States. You could write about weddings, New Year's, Independence Day, or any other special holiday.

Divide your composition into paragraphs. Make the first paragraph a general introduction that tells what you are going to write about. If it is a special holiday, you should give the date and the reason for it in the first paragraph.

In the middle paragraphs, tell about the events of the special day in time order. You may write one, two, or more middle paragraphs. Each middle paragraph should describe a time block.

End your composition with a short concluding paragraph (one or two sentences) that tells why the holiday is important or what it means to you personally.

An outline of your composition might look like this (although the number of paragraphs in the body of your letter may be different):

    I. Introduction
   II. Body
      A. First, . . .
      B . Next, . . .
      C. After that, . . .
      D. Finally, . . .
  III. Conclusion

Hints for Success

- Use time order words and phrases to show the order of events. Use these at the beginnings of some sentences for variety.
- Use adverbs of frequency wherever they are appropriate.
- Use a combination of simple sentences and compound sentences for variety.
- Check your composition carefully for correct punctuation, capitalization, and spelling.

chapter 3

Description

Model: A Day at the Beach

1   It is a beautiful, warm afternoon, and the sun is shining brightly. The wind is blowing, yet it is not cold. There are a lot of people at the beach today. Janice is at the beach with her friends Susan, Tom, and Joey.

      There is a lot of activity on the beach. Many people are taking sunbaths. Janice
5 and Joey are too. Some sunbathers are listening to their radios, and others are reading or sleeping. A fat man is watching a football game on his portable* television set. There is also a group of people playing volleyball. Both teams are yelling and hitting the ball over the net. Everybody is playing hard to win.

      There is a lot of activity in the water, too. Many sailboats are sailing in the
10 distance. Closer to shore, some people are windsurfing on boards with colorful sails. Susan and Tom are in the water. They are swimming to the floating dock.* Some swimmers are sitting on the dock, and others are diving into the water. There are children playing near the water. Some of them are building sand castles. Others are getting their feet wet. Everyone is having a good time.

15   It is one o'clock. Some people are starting to leave, for the weather is beginning to change. The sun isn't shining, nor is the wind blowing gently now. The wind is getting stronger, so it feels cold. Tom and Susan are swimming back to the beach. It is time to go home.

      In conclusion, people are enjoying themselves at the beach today, for there are
20 many things to do.

---

portable: able to be carried around
floating dock: flat platform in the water where swimmers can rest and sunbathe

Questions on the Model

1. Where are Janice and her friends?
2. Who are Janice's friends?
3. What are some people doing?
4. What is the fat man watching?
5. What game is a group of people playing?
6. Where are they hitting the ball?
7. What are some of the people in the water doing?
8. What are Susan and Tom swimming to?
9. What are the children doing?
10. Why are people leaving the beach?

ORGANIZATION

Description: Spatial Order

In chapter 2, you studied chronological order as a way to organize a composition. Chronological order is the arrangement of items in order by time. In this chapter, you will study how to organize a composition using spatial order. **Spatial order** is the arrangement of items in order by space.

Look back at the composition about a day at the beach. This composition uses spatial organization. The introductory paragraph gives general background information to introduce the topic. The second paragraph describes the activities that are happening in one place (on the beach), and the third paragraph describes the activities that are happening in another place (in the water). Each paragraph, therefore, describes a different area of activity. This is spatial organization.

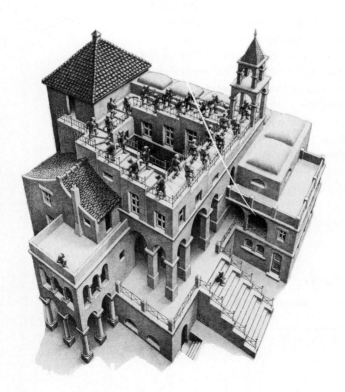

You should use spatial organization mainly when you need to describe something. Suppose you need to describe a painting for an art history class, for example. Look at the following picture. How would you describe it to a blind person?

If you want the blind person to understand the picture, you will use a lot of spatial order expressions in your description so that he or she can follow the movement from one area to another area—right to left, top to bottom, outside to inside, front to back, and so on.

Spatial Order Expressions

Just as there are words and phrases to show time order, there are words and phrases to show spatial arrangement. They are often prepositional phrases of location or position. Some spatial order expressions are

on the beach	in front of	between
in the water	in the front of	behind
in the center	next to	in back of
on the left	around the outside (of)	in the back of

PRACTICE: Spatial Order

Study the following map of Greenhills College, a small private college in the United States. Write sentences telling where the listed places are located. Begin some of your sentences with spatial expressions.

administration building
Parker Hall (classrooms)
the bookstore
the dormitories
the registrar's office
the business office
the admissions office
Galileo Hall (classrooms)
tennis courts
the gymnasium
the post office
the entrance gate
the baseball field
the library
the soccer field
the student cafeteria

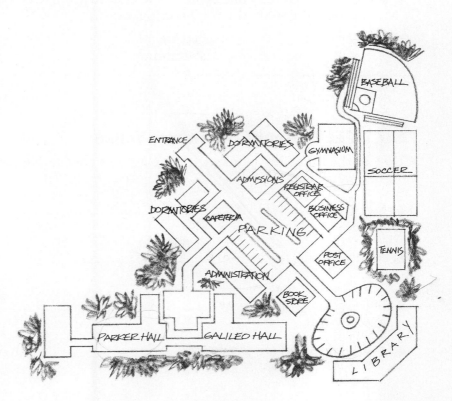

GRAMMAR AND MECHANICS

Present Continuous Tense 時態

The **present continuous tense** is the verb tense used to describe actions that are actually taking place at the present time but that are temporary.

> The sun <u>is shining</u>.
> Many people <u>are taking</u> a sunbath.

RULES FOR PRESENT CONTINUOUS VERB FORMS

When you add *-ing* to a verb to form the present continuous tense, you must know some spelling rules.

- For most verbs, simply add *-ing*:

watch + ing	=	watching
float + ing	=	floating
listen + ing	=	listening
play + ing	=	playing

- If the verb ends in *-e*, drop the *-e*:

take + ing	=	taking
become + ing	=	becoming

- If the verb has only one syllable and ends in a single vowel + single consonant, double the final consonant:

get + ing	=	getting
swim + ing	=	swimming

PRACTICE: Present Continuous Tense

A. Fill in the following blanks with the present continuous form of the verb in <u>parentheses.</u>括弧

1. Some people (listen) _are listening_ to their radios.

2. Many people (take) _are taking_ a sunbath.

3. Both teams (hit) _are hitting_ the ball over the net.

4. Everyone (play) _are playing_ hard to win.

5. Many sailboats (glide*) _____are gliding_____ in the water.

6. Some people (windsurf) _____are windsurfing_____ on boards with colorful sails.

7. Susan (swim) _____is swimming_____ to the floating dock with Tom.

8. Some of the swimmers (sit) _____are sitting_____

   on the dock, and others (dive) _____are diving_____ into the water.

9. One of the children (build) _____is building_____ a sand castle.

10. A few of the children (get) _____are getting_____ their feet wet.

11. Everyone (have) _____is having_____ a good time.

indefinite.

one
each
another
everyone
anyone.

B. Fill in the following blanks with a suitable verb. Use the present continuous verb form.

1   Kitty, Suzy, and Karen _____are studying_____

New York City University. They _____are living_____

in an apartment near the campus.* Today is a rainy day, so the

girls _____are staying_____ home. Suzy

5 _____is sitting_____ on the floor, and she

_____is reading_____ a book. Franklin, the cat,

_____is sleeping_____ on the sofa. Karen

_____is painting_____ a picture of him on her easel.*

Kitty _____is listening_____ to music with her ear-

10 phones.

---

glide: move smoothly
campus: land area of a college, university, or school
easel: wooden frame used by artists to hold a picture while they are painting it

Now the doorbell _____. Karen

stops painting and _____ *walks* _____ to the door.

It's Brad, her fiance, at the door. Suzy and Kitty greet Brad as he

_____ *comes* _____ into the living room. Everybody

15 is happy to see him.

The Subject *it*

It is used in statements about weather, time, distance, and identification. *It* is the subject of the sentence but doesn't have any real meaning.

> Weather:
> It is warm (hot, cold, etc.).
> It is pleasant in the spring.
> It clears up by noon.
> It rains in the summer.
>
> Time:
> It is Sunday.
> It is three o'clock.
>
> Distance:
> It is four hundred miles from San Francisco to Los Angeles.
> It is an hour's drive to the beach from my house.
>
> Identification:
> Who is it? (on the telephone or at the door)
> It's Mary.
> It's my cousin.

CAUTION: Do not confuse *it's* (it + is) with the possessive pronoun *its*, which has no apostrophe.

> It's hot today.
> The book lost its cover.

PRACTICE: *it*

Answer the following questions with sentences that use *it* as the subject.

1. How is the weather today?

It is breezy and warm.

2. When is the party?

It is at 8 o'clock.

3. How long does the trip take?

It is 2 days.

4. How long does it take to get from your home to school?

It is 5 minutes.

5. Who is at the door?

It is Julia

6. How far is it from your house to school?

It is about 30 feet.

7. Who is on the phone?

It is Mike.

8. What time does it clear up?

It is 7 o'clock.

9. What day is the party?

It is on June 14, 1994.

10. How far is it from Earth to the moon?

It's a long way.

The Expletive *there*

There can begin a sentence, but it is not the subject of the sentence. *There*, like *it* in the previous section, has no meaning. The real subject of the sentence comes after *is* or *are*, and the verb must agree with the real subject.

SUBJECT-VERB AGREEMENT RULES

- If the real subject is something uncountable, the verb is singular.

  There is some ice cream in the refrigerator.
  There is a lot of noise in the hall.

- If the real subject is countable and is plural, the verb is plural.

  There are some oranges in the refrigerator.
  There aren't many classes in computer science in the catalogue.

Many sentences beginning with *there is* or *there are* contain expressions of place.

	Real Subject	**Expression of Place**
There is	a lot of activity	on the beach.
There are	children	near the water.

PRACTICE: *there*

A. Fill in the following blanks with *there is* or *there are*.

1. _There are_ some apples in the refrigerator.

2. _There are_ millions of stars in the sky.

3. _There is_ a five-dollar bill on the table.

4. _There are_ ten people waiting in line.

5. _There is_ a lot of noise in this classroom.

6. _There are_ 260 pages in that book.

7. _There is_ no sun today.

8. _There are_ three children in my family.

9. _There is_ someone knocking at the door.

10. _There are_ a lot of people enjoying the beach today.

B. Change the following sentences into sentences beginning with *there is* or *there are*.

1. A video game arcade* is in the shopping center.

   There is a video game arcade in the shopping center.

2. A movie theater is in the shopping center.

   There is a movie theater in the shopping center.

3. Many cars are in the parking lot.

   There are many cars in the parking lot.

---

video game arcade: enclosed place with many video game machines

4. Two public telephones are near the front door.

There are two public telephones near the front door.

5. A soft drink machine is inside of the theater.

There is a soft drink machine inside of the theater.

6. An automatic bank teller machine is outside of the theater.

There is an automatic bank teller machine outside of the theater.

7. A ticket booth is next to the main entrance.

There is a ticket booth next to the main entrance.

8. A good movie is playing in the theater this week.

There is a good movie playing in the theater this week.

9. A lot of people are waiting in line.

There are a lot of people waiting in line.

DICTOCOMP

Write this paragraph as your instructor dictates it to you.

1   My apartment is very small but comfortable. It has a living room, a kitchen, a bedroom, and a bathroom. At the entrance, two doors lead into the bathroom and the bedroom. The bathroom is on the far left, and the bedroom is next to it. Directly in front of the entrance is the kitchen. Between the bedroom and the kitchen
5 is a large storage closet. On the right side of the entrance is the living room. The living room is quite large, for it also serves as a dining room. In the back wall of the living room, a door leads to a narrow balcony. In nice weather, you can sit outside and enjoy the view.

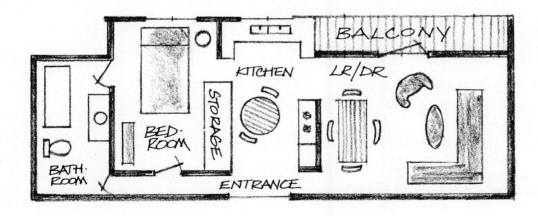

FREEWRITING

Write a paragraph in which you describe the picture on page 40, or cut an interesting picture out of a magazine or newspaper, and describe it. (Attach your picture to your paper when you hand it in.)

Or write a paragraph in which you describe your room at home.

Begin your paragraph with a sentence that names what you are describing and says something interesting about it. Your first sentence might be something like:

As soon as you look at the picture by _____,
you realize that it is not an ordinary drawing.

or

My room has always been a refuge* for me.

Use spatial order expressions in your paragraph. Begin some of your sentences with spatial order expressions ("On the left . . . ," "In the corner . . . ," "In the front of the _____ . . ."). This not only helps organize your spatial description, but it also varies the way you begin sentences and therefore makes your writing more interesting. Begin other sentences with *It is, There is,* and *There are.*

SENTENCE STRUCTURE

Compound Sentences with *yet, for, nor*

You remember from the last chapter that a compound sentence is composed of two simple sentences joined together by a comma and a coordinating conjunction. There are seven coordinating conjunctions in English. In the last chapter, you practiced using *and, but, or* and *so.* In this chapter, you will learn to use the other three: *yet, for,* and *nor.*

RULES FOR USING COORDINATING CONJUNCTIONS

- *yet* has approximately the same meaning as *but;* that is, it shows contrast or joins opposites. We use *yet* most often when the second part of the sentence says something unexpected.

  The wind is blowing, yet it is not cold.
  She didn't love him, yet she married him.

- *for* means *because;* it introduces a reason or cause.

  Some people are starting to leave, for the weather is beginning to change.
  Many people enjoy themselves at the beach on a warm day, for there are many things to do.

---

refuge: place that protects people or animals from danger

▪ *nor* means not this and not that; use *nor* to join two negative sentences.

> The sun isn't shining, nor is the wind blowing now.
> (The sun isn't shining. The wind isn't blowing now.)
> I can't swim well, nor can I play tennis.
> She doesn't like to dance, nor does her boyfriend (like to dance).

NOTE: The word order after *nor* is like a question. The helping verb (*is, does, did, can, will,* etc.) comes before the subject of the part of the sentence introduced by *nor*.

PRACTICE: Compound Sentences with *yet, for, nor*

A. Join the two sentences in each of the following pairs by using a comma and one of these coordinating conjunctions: *yet, for, nor.*

1. Moslems don't drink alcohol. They don't eat pork.

2. Christians are not supposed to work on Sunday. Sunday is their day to worship* God.

3. People who believe in the Hindu religion do not eat beef. They believe that cows are sacred.*

4. Moslem men are permitted to have four wives. Few of them have more than one.

5. Buddhist monks are not married. They may not own property.

B. Make compound sentences from the following incomplete sentences by adding to each a simple sentence that fits the meaning.

1. I have studied English in school for six years, yet _my English havn't very well_.

2. Many children who watch television all day long don't learn how to read, for _the television more interesting than book_.

3. In some countries, women cannot vote, nor _they may not divorce_

---

worship: to pray; to practice religion
sacred: very holy

4. The United States is one of the richest countries in the world, yet

it isn't the biggest land. .

5. Everyone should learn about computers, for _many school or_

company need to use computers. .

C. For additional practice, write two more compound sentences of your own using *nor*.

1. _It's not an animal, nor it can't moved by itself_

_._

2. _She hasn't any job, nor she doesn't worried_
about her life .

ON YOUR OWN!

A. Write a paragraph in which you describe your favorite place. This could be your room at home, a favorite beach, a restaurant, or any place where you feel happy.

In your first sentence, name the place and give a clue as to why you like it. (It's beautiful, restful, exciting, etc.) Then write several sentences describing it very clearly. (Pretend you are describing it to a blind person.) Use spatial order expressions to guide your reader around the place. In your last sentence, make another comment about why it's your favorite place.

★ **B.** Write a composition in which you describe the scene at one of the following places or events: a picnic, a party, a rock music concert, a busy restaurant, a classroom, a library, a chemistry lab, a computer lab, an airport, a subway station, a bar, a disco, a dentist's office, a hospital waiting room, a police station. Use the model composition at the beginning of the chapter as a guide.

In your first paragraph, tell what you are going to describe and give a general picture of the scene in two or three sentences.

In your middle paragraph or paragraphs, divide your place into different areas (on the beach, in the water, etc.) and describe each area in a different paragraph. If your place has only one area, then write only one paragraph in the body of your composition.

In your last paragraph, make a final comment on the place—why you like it, why it is interesting, or what the general mood of the place is.

Hints for Success

- Use a combination of simple and compound sentences for variety.
- Use spatial order expressions to show locations and positions. Use some of these expressions at the beginnings of sentences for variety.
- Use *there is/are* and *it is,* but not at the beginning of every sentence.
- Check your paragraph or composition carefully for correct spelling, capitalization, and punctuation before you hand it in.

PART **II**

Expository Writing

4

Paragraph Organization

You have already been reading and perhaps writing compositions with more than one paragraph in order to increase your writing fluency. Now let's slow down and study the paragraph structure in detail. In this chapter, you will also begin your study of expository writing. Descriptive and narrative writing, which you learned about in the first three chapters, are used to describe things and tell about events. **Expository** writing is used to *explain* things.

Model: A University Professor[1]

1   A university professor has many duties. In the classroom, he or she lectures to the students and answers questions. If the professor is a science instructor, he or she also conducts laboratory experiments. During office hours, students are free to visit the professor to get help on difficult material or problems. In addition, a professor
5 may often work for many hours in a laboratory doing a research project. Another professor might spend his or her time writing a scholarly paper* for a professional journal.* Still another one might spend time writing a book. In conclusion, a professor is always a very busy person. However, he or she usually enjoys his or her work.

WHAT IS A PARAGRAPH?

    A paragraph is a group of related sentences that develops one main idea. As you learned in Chapter 1, each paragraph is a separate unit, marked by indenting the first word from the left-hand margin,* or by leaving extra space above and below the paragraph.

[1]A one-paragraph composition does not need a title because the main idea of the paragraph is given in the first sentence. However, we have used a title to illustrate its purpose and position on the paper.

---

scholarly paper: long, high-level academic essay
journal: magazine   **margin:** space with no printing or writing

Here are some guidelines for correct paragraph form:

1. Write the title in the center of the paper, 1 inch to 1½ inch from the top. The title is only a word or a phrase; it tells the reader what the paragraph is about.
2. Indent the first word of the paragraph as shown in the model.
3. Leave 1-inch margins on both sides and at the bottom of each page.

A paragraph is made up of three kinds of sentences that develop the writer's main idea, opinion, or feeling about a subject. These sentences are (1) the topic sentence, (2) supporting sentences, and (3) the concluding sentence.

In the paragraph you just read, entitled "A University Professor," the first sentence is the **topic sentence.** It tells the reader what the paragraph is about: the activities of a university professor. The seven **supporting sentences** that follow supply the details about the professor's duties. The eighth sentence is the **concluding sentence,** which makes a final statement about the topic and tells the reader that the paragraph is finished. The very last sentence is the writer's comment about the subject.

Now, let's study each part of the paragraph in detail.

THE PARTS OF A PARAGRAPH

The Topic Sentence

The topic sentence is the most general statement of the paragraph. It is the key sentence because it names the subject and the controlling idea: the writer's main idea, opinion, or feeling about that topic.

The topic sentence can come at the beginning or at the end of a paragraph. As a beginning writer, you should write your topic sentence as the first sentence of your paragraph for two reasons. First, it will tell the reader what you are going to say. Second, you can look back at the topic sentence often as you write the supporting sentences. It will help you stick to the subject as you write.

The topic sentence is a complete sentence. It has three parts: a subject, a verb, and a controlling idea.

Determining the **subject** of a topic sentence is a process of narrowing down an idea from general to specific. When your instructor suggests a very general topic, such as college, vacations, or nuclear power, for a writing assignment, you must narrow it down to a limited topic that can be discussed in one paragraph. For example, the topic of college is too general to write about. There are many specific things about college, such as classes, students, teachers, and the campus, that you can discuss. One writer might narrow down the subject of college to the more specific subject of her roommate, Ann.

| college | Lakeview College | dormitory living | roommates | my roommate, Ann |

PRACTICE: Narrowing Subjects from General to Specific

Fill in the space in each funnel until you arrive at a specific subject.
Try to add at least three or four ideas to each group.

audience

1. fashions   **casual clothes**   beachwear   bathing suits   bikini

2. entertainment   **singers**   rock singer   superstar   Madonna

3. sports   **individual sports**   *ball sport*   *basketball*   *basketball star — Magic Johnson*

4. divorce   **children**   *my cousin*   *his grow up*

5. vacations   *go to many countries*   *Europe country*   *Austria*   *Vienna*

6. music   *classical music*   *classical music musicians*   *musician — Beethoven*   *Beethoven wrote the hero syphony.*

The topic sentence of your paragraph must also have a **controlling idea.** The controlling idea is the main point, opinion, or feeling that you have about the subject, and it controls or limits what you will write about it in your paragraph. Putting your ideas in a funnel, as you did in the preceding practice, can help you to arrive at a controlling idea for a topic sentence.

In the example on page 56, the general subject of college has been narrowed to a specific subject, the writer's roommate, Ann. The writer's next step is to decide on a limited area about Ann that can be discussed in one paragraph.

my roommate Ann   **helps me**   English   speaking English

Now that the writer has the subject and a controlling idea, she can write a good, clear topic sentence, which will be her guide as she writes the rest of the paragraph.

Subject	**Controlling Idea**
My roommate, Ann,	helps me to speak English correctly.

PRACTICE: Narrowing Controlling Ideas from General to Specific

In the following practice items, the general idea or subject is given at the widest part of each funnel. Ask yourself questions as you narrow down the ideas: Why...? Who...? What...? Which...? When...? Where...? How...? Add your own ideas to the funnels. Make them more specific as the funnel narrows. Write the most limited idea at the end of the funnel.

1. friends   my best friend   *my best friend—Maggie   her habits   we have the same habits.*

Ask yourself: What do I like about my friend?
                 What do I want to say about him or her?

2. classes   my best/worst class   *English class   reading class   I read a difficult paragraphs*

Ask yourself: Which is my worst/best class?
                 Why?
                 How can I describe it?

3. relationships   *My close relative — my cousin   we grow up and plyied together. -15   Now, he living in Atlanda.*

4. television   *television programs (I like) cartoons   It's describe a magic family- - - - .   Japan*

5. college classes   *Music classes   vocal class teacher- She is very kind and she can understand my mind.*

PRACTICE: Writing Topic Sentences

Write topic sentences using the controlling ideas at the end of the funnels in the preceding exercise. Remember, a topic sentence is a complete sentence. It must have a subject + verb + controlling idea.

Example: Registration at Green Hills College is a frustrating experience.

1. *My best friend - Maggie, because we have the same habits.*
2. *I conquer the English reading class by learning vocabulary. 1st class*
3. *My close relative - my cousin because we grow up together and we like many same things*
4. *My favorite television program in Taiwan is Japan's cartoons - they are so interesting.*
5. *My favorite class in college is vocal class.*

Japanese cartoons are very interesting   I have a perfect vocal teacher because they have many beautiful figures.

PRACTICE: Topic Sentences

A. Study the following pairs of sentences and check the one you think would be a good, clear topic sentence for a paragraph. The first one is done for you.

✓1. Snow skiing on the highest slopes* requires great skill.
  2. Snow skiing is fun.

  3. Exercise is healthful.
✓ **4.** Jogging is beneficial* for several reasons.

  5. Camping is a great outdoor activity.
  6. Camping requires a variety of special equipment.

✓ **7.** The legal age for drinking* should be twenty-one for several reasons.
  8. Drinking is dangerous to your health.

  9. Small cars are popular.
✓**10.** Driving a VW Rabbit is economical*.

11. Hong Kong is an exciting city.
✓**12.** Hong Kong is a shopper's paradise*.

✓**13.** The violence on television can affect children's emotional security*.
14. Watching television is a waste of time.

15. Smoking is a bad habit.
16. It is difficult to quit smoking for three reasons.

B. Improve the following topic sentences. Remember to limit your topic and controlling idea (**be specific**).

  1. I like sports.

    <ins>I like swimming, because</ins>
    <ins>Swimming is beneficial to my body, and lose my weight.</ins>

  2. Safety is important.

    <ins>Safety is our basic need for our life.</ins>

---

slope: side of a mountain
beneficial: good, helpful, useful
drinking: here, drinking alcoholic
  drinks such as beer, wine, or scotch

economical: money-saving
paradise: the best possible place
emotional security: feeling of being safe and loved

3. Small cars are popular.

 Lately, *the* traffice is very busy and clowd, so the small cars are popular. Because small cars are more convvenient and chaper.

4. Exercising is good for everyone.

 Exercising could help my body's circulate, so it's good for everyone.

5. Money is important.

 Becide our health, we can use money to buy everything, "No money No way" So money is important.

C. Write a clear topic sentence about each of the following topics. Remember, the topic sentence is a complete sentence. It must have a subject, a verb, and a controlling idea.

1. a car "No car no foot", *so a* car is very important in my life.

2. a restaurant There are many restaurants in America, because Chinese foot is very famous in the world.

3. English English is very important, we can use it communicate other foreign people.

4. my school or hometown My hometown is Kaohsiung, it's one of biggest in Taiwan.

5. marriage Marriage is very inviolable for Chinese traditional women.

6. being single* Being single *women* are more free than marriage women.

7. a hobby Develop a hobby is very important, because you can use it to keep your part time.

single: not married

Supporting Sentences

The next part of the paragraph is the supporting sentences. They develop the topic sentence by giving specific details about the topic. In order to choose details to support the topic sentence, rephrase it as a question, and then answer that question with your supporting sentences.

For example, in the model paragraph you read about the university professor, the topic sentence is

A university professor has many duties.

If you turn that statement into a question, it will say

What are the duties of a university professor?

The supporting sentences in the paragraph must answer this question by explaining what a professor's duties are. Look back at the model paragraph and complete this list of duties:

1. Lectures to the students.

2. Conducts laboratory experiments.

3. Professor can help students to solve problems in office hours.

4. Professor doing a research project in a laboratory.

5. Another professor must writing a scholarly paper.

6. Inconcrution the professor sebject.

You can see that the supporting sentences list the many duties a professor has.

Another question you can ask about your topic sentence is: How can I prove this? Your supporting sentences should give some facts or examples that prove that your topic sentence is true.

For example, suppose you wrote this topic sentence:

Traditional American family relationships have changed radically* in the last twenty-five years.

You could then ask yourself: How can I prove that this is true? You could prove or support it by giving facts such as these:

1. x out of x marriages end in divorce (in the United States).
2. x out of x children live in homes with only one parent.
3. x percent of couples living together are not legally married.

Still another way to develop your topic sentence is to give examples. Suppose you wrote this topic sentence:

Tokyo is the most expensive city in the world.

radically: very greatly

You could then ask yourself: How can I prove it? You could prove or support this topic sentence by giving examples of the cost of different activities in Tokyo, such as these:

1. Cost of a dinner at a medium-priced restaurant
2. Rent for an average two-bedroom apartment
3. Cost of a ride on public transportation
4. Cost of a medium-priced hotel room

In summary, in order to develop your topic sentence, you must write supporting sentences that prove or support your idea. An easy way to do this is to rephrase your topic sentence as a question *or* to ask yourself: How can I prove this?

PRACTICE: Topic Sentence Questions

First, read each topic sentence. Then, ask a question about the topic. Finally, add two more supporting points to each list.

1. Topic sentence: Smoking in restaurants should be prohibited* for several reasons.

   Question: _Why should smoking should be prohibited in restaurants._

   Supporting points:

   a. It pollutes* the air.
   b. It can affect diners' appetites.
   c. _It makes many butts on the table and on the food._
   d. _It maybe makes a fire._

2. Topic sentence: International students have difficulty taking notes in class for several reasons.

   Question: _Why d_

   Supporting points:

   a. The teacher talks too fast.
   b. The students have poor listening skills.
   c. _The students think that they can remember many detail._
   d. _The students very lazy._
   The teacher uses many difficult words.

prohibited: not allowed   **pollutes:** makes dirty

3. Topic sentence: Women should consider several criteria* before
choosing a sport. *Which idea*

Question: _Why should women consider several_
criteria before choosing a sport?

Supporting points:

  a. They need to decide whether they enjoy exercising alone or
with others.

  b. They need to consider whether they want to enjoy a sport for
recreation.

  c. _They need to choose whether they have ability to do._

  d. _They need to consider whether fit their physically._
                                  they

FREEWRITING

Choose a topic sentence from either Practice B or C on pages 59–60
and write a paragraph of about ten to fifteen sentences about it.

The Concluding Sentence

After you have finished writing the last sentence supporting the
main point of a paragraph, you must end the paragraph with a concluding
sentence. This sentence tells the reader that the paragraph is finished, and
it completes the picture or story about the subject of the paragraph.

The concluding sentence is like the topic sentence because both are
general statements. However, the topic sentence is usually the first
sentence, a general statement that introduces the topic to be discussed in
the paragraph. The concluding sentence is also a general statement, but it
is the last sentence and ends the paragraph.

The concluding sentence reminds the reader of the topic sentence. In
fact, the concluding sentence can be written like the topic sentence but in
different words.

When you write a concluding sentence, you can use one of the
following methods.

- State the topic sentence in different words. **Do not** just copy the
topic sentence.
- Summarize* some (or all) of the main points in the paragraph.

Begin the concluding sentence with a signal phrase that tells the
reader that the paragraph is completed:

    In conclusion, . . .   In summary, . . .

---

criteria: standards for judging something (singular: **criterion**)
summarize: to mention only the most important points

Refer to the model paragraph, "A University Professor." The topic sentence (opening sentence) is

A university professor has many duties.

The concluding sentence (closing sentence) is

In conclusion, a professor is always a very busy person.

It could also be

In summary, a professor has responsibilities both to his students and to his field.

PRACTICE: Writing Concluding Sentences

Write a concluding sentence for each of the following topic sentences. See the preceding examples. Be sure to begin with *In conclusion* or *In summary* (followed by a comma).

1. Learning to write an English paragraph is easy if you follow these steps.

   In conclusion, you follow these steps, you can write an English paragraph.

2. The cafeteria is an inexpensive place to eat.

   In summary, you can choose the cafeteria to eat, because it chaper than another resterant.

3. My first day in school was a frightening experience.

   In conclusion, many first days are frightening experience, but after your first day, you can learn a lot of experience.

4. Everyone in a car should fasten his or her safety belt.

   In summary, everyone in a car should fasten his or her safety belt, it can safeguard your life.

5. Watching television is a good way to learn English conversation.

___

The Concluding Comment

After the concluding sentence of a paragraph, you may add a **concluding comment.** This sentence is the writer's final comment or thought about the subject of the paragraph. The purpose of the final comment is to give the reader something to think about and to remember about the paragraph. In the following example, the second sentence is the writer's final comment about a university professor.

In conclusion, a professor is always a very busy person. However, she or he usually enjoys her or his work.

PRACTICE: Concluding Comments

The following scrambled groups of sentences include a topic sentence, a concluding sentence, and a concluding comment. Study each group carefully, and underline the concluding comment sentence in each.

1. You can lose weight if you follow these steps. It will take both time and effort, but the results will make you happy. Losing weight is not difficult.

2. Everyone should be aware of the dangers of heavy smoking. Smoking is the cause of several serious diseases. Smoking can harm important organs* of the body.

3. A working couple should divide home responsibilities. By sharing the work, they will have more time for leisure* activities. A husband should be willing to help his wife with the children, housework, and shopping.

4. It is important for consumers to be aware of the dangers of such false advertising. These advertisements carry the message that young people can smoke and still be good looking, healthy, and athletic. Cigarette advertisements try to attract young people in several ways.

5. Take the boredom out of exercising and do it to music. Exercising to music can increase your enthusiasm. Listening to fast-tempo* music while running or aerobic* dancing will make exercising easier and fun.

PREWRITING ACTIVITIES

Before you can write a well-organized paragraph with good supporting sentences, you need to do some prewriting activities.

Step 1: Brainstorm

Brainstorming is a prewriting activity in which you write down any ideas or feelings you have about the subject of your topic sentence. Do it this way:

1. Write down your topic sentence.
2. Make a list of everything that comes to your mind about the subject. (Don't worry about the controlling idea for now.)
3. Forget about order of ideas, grammar, structure, or spelling. (Use words, phrases, and/or sentences.)
4. Just keep writing down whatever comes to your mind until you run out of ideas.

---

organs: parts of the body such as lungs, heart, stomach
leisure: free time

fast-tempo: with a fast beat
aerobic: exercising the heart

In the following example, the writer has put down many ideas about the topic, Rita, in no particular order, without worrying about grammar, punctuation, or the controlling idea.

Topic sentence: Rita, my roommate, is very inconsiderate*.

1. kitchen in a mess
2. she wears heavy makeup
3. loves soap operas
4. uses the bathroom for an hour every morning
5. it's always in a mess
6. fast food freak*
7. eats my food
8. conceited*
9. my phone messages—seldom takes
10. drives me to work—sometimes

Then, the writer goes back over the list and crosses out any ideas that don't prove or support the topic sentence. As you go over each point on your list, ask yourself this question: Will this point support the controlling idea?

In the example topic sentence, the controlling idea is that Rita is inconsiderate. Let's evaluate the points on the brainstorming list.

1. Rita leaves the kitchen in a mess.
Will this point prove that Rita is inconsiderate?
Since the answer is yes, leave it in.

2. She wears heavy makeup.
This will not support the controlling idea, so cross it out.

Remember, the writer must test each point to see whether or not it will prove the controlling idea that Rita is inconsiderate.

Step 2: List Your Supporting Points

The next step in prewriting is to list the points that you will use in the paragraph. Remember, all of them must support the controlling idea of the topic sentence. In our example, the controlling idea is that Rita is inconsiderate. The writer can use these supporting points:

1. leaves the kitchen in a mess
2. uses the bathroom for over an hour every morning
3. leaves it in a mess
4. eats my food
5. seldom takes my phone messages

---

inconsiderate: not aware of other people's feelings
fast food freak: person who loves food from places such as McDonald's (slang)
conceited: having a too-high opinion of oneself

The supporting points should be listed in the order in which you will write about them. Keep the same ideas together. In our example, points 1 and 4 should go together (kitchen and food); points 2 and 3 should go together (bathroom); and point 5 (telephone) should come last.

Step 3: Make a Simple Outline

The outline is a helpful guide for you to use as you write your paragraph. In an outline you list the main points in the order in which you will write about them. This will help you to organize thoughts. To help you to stay with the topic, look at your outline as you write your paragraph. The following is a simple outline form:

I. Topic sentence
II. Supporting sentences
  A. Main supporting sentence 1
  B. Main supporting sentence 2
  C. Main supporting sentence 3
         Etc.
III. Concluding sentence

Based on this simple model, our example paragraph about Rita could be outlined like this:

I. Rita, my roommate, is very inconsiderate.
II. A. She leaves the kitchen in a mess.
    B. She eats my food.
    C. She uses the bathroom for over an hour every morning.
    D. She always leaves it in a mess.
    E. She seldom takes my phone messages.
III. In conclusion, Rita is a very thoughtless person.

A more detailed outline would look like this:

I. Topic sentence
II. Supporting sentences
  A. First main supporting sentence
    1. Supporting detail 1
    2. Supporting detail 2
    3. Supporting detail 3
  B. Second main supporting sentence
    1. Supporting detail 1
    2. Supporting detail 2
    3. Supporting detail 3
  C. Third main supporting sentence
    1. Supporting detail 1
    2. Supporting detail 2
    3. Supporting detail 3
         Etc.
III. Concluding sentence

In this outline, main supporting sentences A, B, and C are the major points of the paragraph. Each one of them supports the topic sentence. Supporting details 1, 2, and 3 are the supporting details for each of the major points.

△ Based on this more detailed model, our example paragraph about Rita could be outlined like this:

I. Rita, my roommate, is very inconsiderate.
II. A. She leaves the kitchen in a mess.
    1. Food out
    2. Dirty sink
  B. She eats my food.
    1. Red apple
    2. Milk
  C. She uses the bathroom for over an hour every morning.
    1. Shower routine
    2. Makeup
  D. She always leaves the bathroom in a mess.
    1. Dirty towels
    2. Toothpaste
  E. She seldom takes my phone messages.
    1. Poor memory
    2. No written messages
III. In conclusion, Rita is a very thoughtless person. If she doesn't change some of her ways soon, I am going to look for another roommate.

WRITING THE PARAGRAPH

After you have done the prewriting activities, you are ready to write a good paragraph. Use the outline as a guide for writing the paragraph. Begin the paragraph with the topic sentence. Develop each main point and its supporting details in the paragraph in the order in which they are written in the outline.

Here is our example paragraph about Rita, finally written in paragraph form. The topic sentence is in **bold** type. The main supporting sentences are <u>underlined</u>. The concluding sentence is in **bold** type.

My Roommate Rita

1   **Rita, my roommate, is very inconsiderate.** <u>She leaves the kitchen in a mess.</u> Yesterday, Rita made a sandwich and left the lettuce and mayonnaise on the breadboard. Also, she frequently leaves one or two dirty pots or pans in the sink. Sometimes she eats my food without asking. Last week, she ate the red apple

5   that I was going to take for lunch. This morning she used up my milk on her breakfast cereal. <u>Besides, Rita uses the bathroom for an hour or more every morning.</u> She showers, and washes and blowdries her hair. She even makes up her face in there. <u>Of course, the bathroom is always in a mess.</u> I have found towels on the floor and toothpaste on the washbasin. She even leaves her dirty laundry on the

10   towel racks. <u>Finally, she seldom takes my phone messages.</u> Last night, I asked her if anyone had called while I was out. But she couldn't remember if Jim or Joe had called. When she does take a message, she sometimes forgets to write down an important phone number. **In conclusion, Rita is a very thoughtless person.** If she doesn't change some of her ways soon, I am going to look for another roommate.

PRACTICE: Understanding the Paragraph

Let's review the paragraph about Rita to make sure you understand its structure. The first sentence is the topic sentence. It introduces the topic and the controlling idea for the whole paragraph.

Rita, my roommate, is very inconsiderate.

All of the main supporting sentences that follow the topic sentence must support it. Notice that each of the main supporting sentences has a main idea. So, for example, the first main supporting sentence points out one of the writer's main complaints.

She leaves the kitchen in a mess.

The supporting details prove this statement by explaining that food is left out and that the kitchen sink is left dirty. So, this part of the paragraph is now complete.

The second main supporting sentence also supports the topic sentence, by pointing out another of the writer's main complaints.

> Sometimes she eats my food without asking.

Again, the supporting details must explain this main point. Both the apple and the milk have disappeared. These details complete this section of the paragraph.

Now, in the following blanks, add the supporting details for the rest of the main supporting sentences in the paragraph about Rita.

Third supporting sentence:

Rita uses the bathroom for an hour or more every morning.

1. _She showers, and washes and blowdries her hair._
2. _She (even) makes up her face in there._ _{also portion}

Fourth supporting sentence:

The bathroom is always in a mess.

1. _I have found towels on the floor and toothpaste on the washbasin._
2. _She even leaves her dirty laundry on the towel racks._

Fifth supporting sentence:

She seldom takes my phone messages.

1. _Last night, I asked her if anyone had called while I was out._
2. _But she couldn't even remember if Jim or Joe had called._
3. _When she does take a message, she sometimes forgets to write down an important phone number._

ON YOUR OWN!

Write a one-paragraph composition in which you describe (1) a good or bad habit of one of your friends or family members, or (2) your pet dog or cat.

Hints for Success

- Do the prewriting activities:
  1. Brainstorm.
  2. List your supporting points.
  3. Write a simple outline.

  Then, write your paragraph from your outline.
- Vary your sentence openings. (Don't always start with the subject.)
- Use a combination of simple and compound sentences for variety.
- Check your paragraph carefully for spelling, capitalization, and punctuation.

chapter 5

More about Paragraph Organization

Model: Arranged Marriages

1   Choosing a husband or wife is one of the most important decisions in a person's life because a good marriage can mean the difference between a happy and an unhappy life. In many cultures, young men and women choose their own marriage partners. In some cultures, on the other hand, parents arrange their children's
5 marriages. Such arranged marriages have both advantages and disadvantages.

One advantage to having parents arrange a marriage is financial security. Of course, money doesn't automatically* bring happiness, but a lack of money certainly causes stress* in any relationship. A second advantage of an arranged marriage is that parents may make a better choice than their children. They are not
10 only older but also wiser. Also, parents have been married; therefore, they know better what qualities are desirable in a spouse*. Furthermore, parents may be better judges of character than young people, who often let emotions influence* their judgment. To summarize, arranged marriages may be happy because parents choose with their heads, not with their hearts.

15   On the other hand, arranged marriages may have some disadvantages. One obvious* disadvantage is that parents may make a poor choice, and the young couple may never be happy together. A second obvious disadvantage is that a young man or woman may already have fallen in love with someone else. If the parents force him or her to marry their choice, the result will be *three* unhappy
20 people.

In conclusion, neither an arranged marriage nor a marriage for love is necessarily going to be happy. Both kinds of marriages take work, patience, and perhaps a little bit of luck.

---

automatically: without effort
stress: pressure on a person caused
    by outside problems
spouse: husband or wife
influence: power over someone's mind
obvious: easy to understand, clear without explanation

Questions on the Model

1. What is an arranged marriage?
2. In your culture, do parents (or other relatives) arrange their children's marriages?
3. How many advantages of an arranged marriage does the author discuss? What are they?
4. What two disadvantages of an arranged marriage does the author mention?
5. Which system of marriage do you think is better—marriage for love or arranged marriage? Why?

SENTENCE STRUCTURE

In the first three chapters, you learned about simple and compound sentences. In this chapter, we will review what you already know and add a little information about compound sentences. Then we will introduce you to a third kind of English sentence, complex sentences.

Independent Clauses

A **clause** is a group of words containing a subject and a verb. Some clauses can stand alone as a sentence. This kind of clause is an **independent clause.** A simple sentence is one independent clause.

> Tom loves Erica.

A compound sentence is two independent clauses joined together by a comma and one of the seven coordinating conjunctions: *and, but, so, or, nor, for, yet.*

> Tom loves Erica, and she loves him.
> Jack loves Jean, but she loves Ronald.
> Jack should forget Jean, or he will die a lonely man.
> Jean doesn't love Jack, so she won't marry him.

Another way to make a compound sentence is to join the two independent clauses with a semicolon. Notice that the first word after a semicolon is not capitalized.

> Tom loves Erica; she loves him.
> Jack loves Jean; she loves Ronald.
> Jean doesn't love Jack; she won't marry him.

NOTE: *Or* cannot be replaced by a semicolon.

A third way to make a compound sentence is to join the two independent clauses with a semicolon + sentence connector + comma. A sentence connector is a word such as *however* or *therefore.*

Here is a list of frequently used sentence connectors and their approximate meanings.

Sentence Connector	Meaning
moreover	and
furthermore	and
however	but
otherwise	or, in the sense of "if not"
therefore	so, in the sense of "as a result"

Tom loves Erica; moreover, she loves him.
Tom loves Erica; furthermore, she loves him.
Jack loves Jean; however, she loves Ronald.
Jack should forget Jean; otherwise, he will die a lonely man.
Jean doesn't love Jack; therefore, she won't marry him.

PRACTICE: Compound Sentences

Combine each of the following pairs of sentences to make a compound sentence. Use all three ways you have just learned, and punctuate carefully.

1. Robots can do boring, repetitive work. They can do unsafe jobs.

a. _____

b. _____

c. _____

2. Robots can make minor decisions. They cannot really think.

a. _____

b. _____

c. _____

3. Robots don't get tired, sick, or hungry. They can work twenty-four hours a day.

a. _____

b. _____

c. _____

4. Human factory workers must learn new skills. They will be out of work because of robots.

a. _____

b. (not possible)

c. _____

Dependent Clauses

A **dependent clause** is a clause (a group of words with a subject and a verb) that does not express a complete thought and cannot stand alone. There are different kinds of dependent clauses:

- dependent adjective clauses

  which is celebrated on May 1st
  whose child was kidnapped

- dependent adverb clauses

  before he died
  because she loved him

- dependent noun clauses

  that we could go
  whether it was raining

A dependent clause *must* be connected to an independent clause in order to make a complete sentence, which is called a **complex sentence.**

Independent Clause	Dependent Clause
An important holiday in Russia is May Day,	which is celebrated on May 1st.
I feel sorry for the couple	whose child was kidnapped.
He had only one wish	before he died.
She married him	because she loved him.

The word that begins a dependent clause is called a **subordinating conjunction.** In the examples you just read, the subordinating conjunctions are *which, whose, before,* and *because.* The first two signal a dependent adjective clause, and the last two signal a dependent adverb clause. We will study adverb clauses in this chapter and adjective and noun clauses in later chapters.

PRACTICE: Dependent and Independent Clauses

A. Write *independent* or *dependent* in front of each of the following clauses:

————————————— **1.** When we arrived at the airport two hours later.

————————————— **2.** We arrived at the airport two hours later.

————————————— **3.** Because the teacher gave such hard exams.

————————————— **4.** After they got married.

————————————— **5.** Afterward, they got married.

————————————— **6.** Which is not an easy thing to do.

————————————— **7.** Which student got the highest grade?

————————————— **8.** Whose sunglasses are these?

————————————— **9.** While I was a student in high school.

————————————— **10.** Where he parked his car.

B. Write *complete* if the sentence is complete, or *incomplete* if it is not:

————————————— **1.** Because it was snowing when we woke up.

————————————— **2.** A woman whom I admire.

————————————— **3.** I will meet him before noon.

————————————— **4.** Before she left for Tokyo.

————————————— **5.** Although I knew the answer to all the questions.

————————————— **6.** When did you get your driver's license?

————————————— **7.** Before you get your driver's license.

————————————— **8.** The park where we had a picnic was crowded.

————————————— **9.** Where we last saw her standing in the rain.

————————————— **10.** Since I haven't heard from them for a month.

Complex Sentences with Adverb Clauses

Dependent **adverb clauses** tell *why, when,* or *where,* or introduce an opposite idea. They begin with one of these subordinating conjunctions:

- To tell why: *because, since, as*

  because she was the youngest child
  since she was the youngest child
  as she was the youngest child

- To tell when and where: *when, whenever, since, while, after, before, wherever*

  when he first met her
  whenever he remembered her smile
  since he first saw her
  while he was waiting for a taxi
  after he heard her voice
  before he realized it
  wherever he went

- To introduce an opposite idea: *although, though, even though*

  although she is an athlete
  though she is an athlete
  even though she is an athlete

A complex sentence with an adverb clause consists of an independent clause + an adverb clause. You may write the clauses in either order:

- Pattern 1: independent clause + dependent clause

  She smokes heavily even though she is an athlete.

- Pattern 2: dependent clause + independent clause

  Even though she is an athlete, she smokes heavily.

COMMA RULE

In a complex sentence, if the dependent clause comes first, put a comma after it.

PRACTICE: Complex Sentences with Adverb Clauses

A. In the following sentences, underline independent clauses with a solid line and dependent clauses with a broken line. In addition, draw a circle around subordinating conjunctions.

1. (Although) you may not believe it, the following is a true story.

2. One cold morning in January 1800, a man in a small village in France noticed a strange-looking boy in his garden when he went outside.

3. The boy seemed more like an animal than a human because he was dressed in rags*, had scars all over his body, and could not speak.

4. Before he was found, he had lived in the forest with wild animals.

5. He ate with his hands and tore off clothes whenever anyone tried to dress him.

6. He didn't seem to feel heat because he put his hands directly into a fire to get food.

7. Because he always tried to run away, his keepers took him for walks on a leash, like a dog.

8. After a while, he was sent to a city where he was put in a school for deaf children.

9. After he had been at the school for several years, he went to live with a kind woman in her home.

10. He never learned to speak even though he lived among humans for more than twenty-five years.

11. Since the first "wild boy" was found, there have been others.

12. When two girls were discovered living in a cave with wolf cubs in India, they acted just like the wolves.

13. One girl died after she was captured, although the other girl lived for nine years and even learned to speak.

B. Add an independent clause to each dependent adverb clause in the list on page 78. In some sentences, put the dependent clause first. In others, put it last.

Example: because she was the youngest child

Her father spoiled her because she was the youngest child.

or

Because she was the youngest child, her father spoiled her.

---

rags: old, worn-out clothes

ORGANIZATION

Unity

It is important for a paragraph to have **unity.** When a paragraph has unity, all of the sentences in it discuss only *one* idea. In the model essay, for example, the second paragraph discusses only the *advantages* of arranged marriages; it has unity. The third paragraph also has unity because it discusses only the *disadvantages*. Notice also that only arranged marriages are discussed in these two paragraphs. To discuss any other kind of marriage system would destroy the essay's unity.

Remember: All of the sentences in a paragraph must discuss the same idea. If you start to discuss a new idea, start a new paragraph.

PRACTICE: Unity

A. Find and cross out any sentences that do not belong in the paragraphs below.

1. Chinese Food

1   Chinese food is popular everywhere in the world. Most people would agree that Chinese cuisine* is especially flavorful, varied, and healthful. Not even the best French chefs can equal the imaginative combination of ingredients and delicious blend of flavors of Chinese cooking. Japanese
5 food is more beautiful to look at than Chinese food.

2. New Sports

1   As people have more time and money to spend on recreation, new sports are developed. Traditional sports such as racing—on foot, horses, and skis, and in boats, cars, and airplanes—are still popular. Fifteen years ago, no one had ever heard of windsurfing. Now it is the rage* at beach resorts
5 everywhere. Twenty years ago, who would have thought that intelligent men and women would jump out of airplanes for fun, as they do in the sport of skydiving? Ten years ago, not many people believed that humans would be able to glide through the air like birds, as they do in the new sport of hang gliding.

B. The following short essay should have four paragraphs. Decide where each new paragraph should begin and mark the place with a double slash.

Predicting Earthquakes

1   On July 28, 1976, a giant earthquake struck near Tangphan, China. It measured 8.2 on the Richter scale and killed 800,000 people. Such terrible tragedies could be avoided if scientists could predict earthquakes accurately —that is, tell when they will happen *before* they happen. At present, however,
5 the two most reliable means of earthquake prediction give only a few hours'

---

cuisine: style of cooking   **rage:** something that is in fashion (slang)

warning. First of all, seismographs, which are instruments to record and measure earthquakes, can also show when they will happen. They record the different kinds of waves, called *S*-waves and *P*-waves, that are sent out when the earth vibrates, or moves. Scientists have learned that *P*-waves slow down

10 for a while and then speed up just before an earthquake. Thus, seismographs can predict earthquakes, but only a few hours beforehand. A second way to predict earthquakes is to watch animal behavior. Scientists have learned that dogs, chickens, horses, and other animals often behave in unusual ways before an earthquake. They run around excitedly and act afraid. Scientists

15 think that animals can sense earth vibrations long before humans can. Again, however, there is only a few hours' notice. To summarize, scientists are learning to predict earthquakes using both scientific instruments and animal behavior. Let us hope that their work will help prevent great numbers of deaths when killer quakes strike in the future.

Coherence

In addition to unity, every good paragraph in a composition must have **coherence.** One way to achieve coherence is through the use of transition signals.

Transition signals are words and phrases that connect the idea in one sentence with the idea in another sentence. They are expressions like *first/second, moreover, however, in brief,* and so on. They make the movement between sentences in a paragraph smooth so the reader does not have problems understanding the writer's ideas. Transition signals are also used in multi-paragraphed compositions to make the movement from one paragraph to the next logical and smooth.

Read the following compositions. Is A or B easier to understand? Why?

Composition A

1   Americans are crazy about* their pet dogs. They do many things for them. They treat their pets like human beings. They like to talk to their dogs and treat them like children. My neighbor Mrs. Green talks to her dog Ruffy all the time. She takes him for a walk twice a day. She will not leave him when he is sick. Americans send

5   their dogs to training school to learn to be good.

Americans spend a lot of money on their pets. They feed them expensive dog food with flavors that people like such as beef, chicken, liver, and cheese. Their pets have brightly colored balls, rubber bones, and other toys to play with. In the winter, it is not unusual to see dogs with coats on to keep warm. Some dogs even wear

10 collars with colorful, sparkling stones that look like diamonds or rubies. Some owners bathe their dogs in the bathtub. Others take their pets to a dog beauty shop. Their toenails are clipped. Their fur is brushed and trimmed. They are given a bath with special dog shampoo. This beauty treatment costs about twenty-five dollars.

(to be) crazy about: to like or love something very much (idiom)

15   Americans love their pet dogs a lot. They are willing to spend both time and money on them. They believe that "a dog is man's best friend." Dogs are loyal and dependable and wonderful companions.

Composition B

1   Americans are crazy about their pet dogs, so they do many things for them. First of all, they treat their pets like human beings. They like to talk to their dogs and treat them like children. For example, my neighbor Mrs. Green talks to her dog Ruffy all the time. Also, she takes him for a walk twice a day and will not leave him
5   when he is sick. Moreover, Americans send their dogs to training school to learn to be good.

   Second, Americans spend a lot of money on their pets. They feed them expensive dog food with flavors that people like such as beef, chicken, liver, and cheese. Also, their pets have brightly colored balls, rubber bones, and other toys to
10   play with. Some dogs even wear collars with colorful, sparkling stones that look like diamonds or rubies. Some owners bathe their dogs in the bathtub, while others take their pets to a dog beauty shop. First, their toenails are clipped. Then, their fur is brushed and trimmed. Finally, they are given a bath with special dog shampoo. This beauty treatment costs about twenty-five dollars.

15   In conclusion, because Americans love their pet dogs a lot, they are willing to spend both time and money on them. They believe that "a dog is man's best friend" because dogs are loyal and dependable and wonderful companions.

   Composition B is easier to read and understand because the writer has used transition signals. Each transition signal shows the relationship of one sentence to another. Let's review the transition signals in Composition B.

- *So* tells you the result (or effect) of the first clause or sentence.
- *First of all* tells you this is the first thing that Americans do for their dogs.
- *Second* tells you this is the second thing Americans do for their dogs.
- *For example* tells you that an example of the preceding statement(s) will follow.
- *Moreover, also* tell you that an idea related to the one you just read is coming.
- *First, then, finally* tell you the time order of the dog's beauty treatment.
- *In conclusion* tells you that this is the end of the essay.

It is important to use transition signals as you write to connect one sentence with another or to introduce each new paragraph of a composition. You should learn to use them correctly. The following is a chart of some of the most common transition signals.

TRANSITION SIGNALS

| Usage | Sentence Connectors | Conjunctions | |
		Coordinating	Subordinating
To list ideas in time order or order of importance	first (second, etc.) first of all then, next, finally		
To add another idea	furthermore in addition moreover	and	
To add an opposite idea	on the other hand however	but	although even though
To add a similar idea	similarly likewise also	and	
To give an example	for example for instance		
To give a cause (or reason)		for	because since as
To give an effect (or result)	therefore consequently	so	
To add a conclusion	in conclusion in brief		

Let's review how coordinators, sentence connectors, and subordinators are used to combine sentences.

Coordinators (coordinating conjunctions) make compound sentences from two independent clauses:

Independent clause, *and* / *or* / *but* / *for* / *so* / *yet* / *nor* + independent clause.

I like to swim, but I don't like to jog.
Swimming is good exercise, so I swim everyday.

Some **sentence connectors** can be used with a semicolon and a comma to join two independent clauses into a compound sentence, **or** they can be used at the beginning of a sentence with a comma only.

Independent clause; *furthermore,* / *in addition,* / *moreover,* / *also,* / *therefore,* / *consequently,* / *on the other hand,* / *however,* + independent clause.

I dislike jogging; therefore, I never do it.
or
I dislike jogging. Therefore, I never do it.

Other sentence connectors can only be used at the beginning of a sentence and are followed by a comma.

In conclusion,
In brief, + sentence.

In conclusion, everyone should exercise regularly.

First,
First of all,
Second,
Third, + sentence.
Then,
Next,
Finally,

First, bend at the waist, touch the floor, and count five.
Second, raise your body slowly.
Then, raise your hands above your head and count five.
Finally, drop your arms to your sides.
Repeat the above exercises six times.

Subordinators (subordinating conjunctions) are the first words in dependent clauses. A dependent clause must be added to an independent clause to make a complex sentence. Remember that the clauses can be in either order. If the dependent clause is first, put a comma after it.

Pattern 1:

Independent Clause + *although* dependent clause.
                   when
                   because

    I exercise every day although I hate it.
    Walking is good for you because it exercises the heart.

Pattern 2:

Although
When   dependent clause, + independent clause.
Because

    Because I have gained ten pounds, the doctor ordered me to get into an exercise program.

PRACTICE: Transition Signals

A. Read the model composition on page 73 and underline all the transition signals. Refer to the chart on page 83 if you need help.

B. In the following composition, choose an appropriate transition signal from those listed after each blank and write it in the blank. In some cases there may be more than one appropriate answer. Capitalize and punctuate correctly.

How Storms are Named

1   Have you ever wondered how those big ocean storms called hurricanes or typhoons get their names? Who decides to name a hurricane "Ann" or "Barbara" or "Bill"? The way hurricanes and typhoons are named has changed over the years and is an interesting story.

5   _____ (first, initially, originally) weather forecasters described them by their position in degrees of latitude and longitude _____ (in addition, for example, since) a typhoon might be called "21.20 north, 157.52 west" _____ (then, however, moreover) this method was confusing because storms don't stay in the same

10 place _____ (thus, therefore, in conclusion) people developed other ways to identify them. In the Caribbean Ocean, hurricanes were named for the Catholic saints' days _____ (therefore, for example, moreover) a hurricane that struck an island in the Caribbean on Saint Ann's Day was named "Santa Ana." A weather forecaster in Australia

15 used to name typhoons after politicians whom he disliked _____ (so, for example, however) he could make weather forecasts such as "Typhoon Smith is on a very destructive path" or "Typhoon Jones is very weak

and is not moving in any direction." _____ (in addition, later, as a result) during World War I, hurricanes and typhoons were named
20 according to the military alphabet: Able, Baker, Charlie, etc. _____ (later, then, furthermore) during World War II, women's names began to be used _____ (so, therefore, and) for the next thirty-five years, weather forecasters talked about "Typhoon Alice" or "Hurricane Betsy." _____ (however, then, in
25 addition) in the 1970s, the women's liberation movement came along and forced weather forecasters to use men's names, too. _____ (thus, for example, finally), after about 1975, a storm could be named "Gertrude" or "George." _____ (in conclusion, so, as a result) the way hurricanes
30 and typhoons are named has changed over the years and will undoubtedly change again.

Another way to achieve coherence in writing is through the writer's consistent* choice of such elements as person (I, he, she, they, you, one), voice (active or passive), and register (formal or informal).

The following paragraph is not consistent in person. As you read the paragraph, notice how the subjects of the sentences change from "a student" to "they" to "you."

Incoherent Paragraph:

A *student* who knows a few Latin and Greek roots and prefixes has an advantage over a student who doesn't know them. *They* can often guess the meaning of unfamiliar words. If, for example, *you* know that the prefix "*circum-*" means "around," *you* can guess the meaning of words such as *circumference*, *circumvent*, *circumstance*, and *circumnavigate* when *you* read them in a sentence.

---

consistent: the same, not changing

In the following paragraph, the problem has been corrected. The subject nouns and pronouns are consistent, and the paragraph has coherence.

Coherent Paragraph:

Students who know a few Latin and Greek roots and prefixes have an advantage over students who don't know them. They can often guess the meaning of unfamiliar words. If, for example, they know that the prefix *circum-* means "around," they can guess the meaning of words such as *circumference, circumvent, circumstance, and circumnavigate* when they read them in a sentence.

Remember: Be consistent! If you use the pronoun *I* at the beginning of your paragraph, keep it throughout. If you begin with a singular noun such as *a student* or singular pronouns such as *he, she,* or *it,* don't change to plural *the students* or *they.*

PRACTICE: Coherence

A. In each of the following paragraphs, circle the noun or pronoun that is the topic of the paragraph and all of the pronouns that refer to it.

1. Sound requires a definite time to travel from one place to another. The speed of sound in air depends on wind conditions, temperature, and humidity. Sound travels faster through warm air than through cold air. It travels about four times faster in water than it does in air.

2. I am developing a burning desire to achieve my goal. I have written down what my principal objective is, and I repeat it to myself frequently. In addition, I have become more organized and efficient. I even study during vacations and, of course, on a regular schedule during the school year. I know what I want, and I am looking forward to achieving my goal.

3. An Olympic athlete must be strong not only in body, but also in mind. She or he has to train for years to achieve the necessary strength and control over her or his sport to compete in the Olympics. This requires great discipline and self-sacrifice. Similarly, the Olympic athlete has to train her or his mind in order to compete under extreme mental pressure. This, too, requires great discipline. In other words, an Olympic athlete must be in top condition, both mentally and physically.

B. The following paragraphs lack coherence because the subject noun or pronoun changes within the paragraph. Correct the inconsistent words by making the subjects consistent in person and number. If necessary, change the verbs to make them agree with their new subjects.

1. Physicists are scientists who are involved in the discovery of the basic laws of nature and the application of these laws to improve the world. They are concerned with phenomena* as large as the universe or as small as an electron. A physicist is a problem solver who is curious about the universe and who is interested in what gives it order and meaning.

---

phenomena: facts or events (singular: **phenomenon**)

2. Many students feel that learning to write well is a useless, time-consuming task that has little to do with "real life"—that is, with their future occupations. While this may be true if he or she plans to become an auto mechanic or a waitress, it is certainly not true if you plan to have a white-collar job. No matter what profession you enter—business, engineering, government—you will have to write.

3. Of course, a professional writing assignment is not called a composition. Instead, they are called by many different names: business letters, marketing studies, procedure manuals, and so on.

4. However, the process for writing a composition and, for example, a business report, is very similar. First, you collect information. Then, the information is organized into an outline. Next, the writer writes the report or composition. After that, it is edited and revised. Finally, you are ready to type it and submit it to your boss or teacher.

(NOTE: Paragraph 4 is more difficult to correct because it contains both active and passive sentences. If you do not know the difference between active and passive, do not do paragraph 4.)

THE WRITING PROCESS

Many students have the mistaken idea that a composition needs to be written only once in rough draft form, then rewritten to be handed in. This is simply not true. Unfortunately, writing is not such a simple process. Even professional writers rewrite and rewrite and rewrite because it takes many attempts to produce the perfect, finished copy that clearly communicates their ideas.

When you sit down to write a paragraph or an essay, you start with an idea or assignment. You must then write down on paper your thoughts about the subject. Your ideas must be organized clearly and logically*, and your sentences must flow smoothly. You may be wondering how you can produce such a perfect composition. It certainly is possible. However, in order to write well, you must be prepared to rewrite your paper several times before you end up with a paper that clearly communicates what you want to say. There is no shortcut.

When writing your first draft, be sure to leave space between lines of writing and on the sides of the paper so you can write in any new thoughts or correct what you have already written. Use a pencil (not a pen) to make changes. Draw a single line through the old material so that it is still readable because after thinking about it again, you may want to use it after all.

The key to writing well is a simple process called **revision.** You must write several drafts of your paper. While you are rereading your rough drafts, you must question what you have written.

In the process of revision, you read through your piece of writing to make improvements and also to correct mistakes. You can change a word,

---

logically: reasonably, intelligently

a phrase, a part of or a complete sentence, or an entire paragraph, and you can also reorder your paragraphs. You may even decide to change the entire essay. While you are making changes in your composition, you are also thinking about ways to improve the organization and development in order to make your composition clearer and easier to understand.

Always keep in mind that writing is a process of discovery. As you are writing, you will come up with ideas that may not be on your brainstorming list or outline. Remember that nothing you have written is final. It is perfectly fine to add new ideas or to throw out old ones at any point in the writing process.

Whenever you write, we suggest that you use the following plan of writing, revising, rewriting, refining, rewriting, and perfecting each paragraph.

The First Draft: Organization and Development

Read over your first draft carefully to make sure that you have developed your ideas well enough so the reader clearly understands your position on the subject. Use these questions as a checklist:

- Have you written a clear topic sentence with a controlling idea?
- Have you used enough details and examples to support the topic sentence?
    - Add additional supporting details or examples to make your paragraph stronger.
- Does each paragraph have unity?
    - Draw a line through any sentence that does not support the topic sentence.
- Does your paragraph have coherence?
    - Can your reader follow your ideas and understand what you have written?
    - Have you used appropriate transition signals to connect your ideas?
    - Have you used the correct pronouns that refer back to key nouns?

After you have checked these points, you are ready to write your second draft.

The Second Draft: Grammar and Mechanics

As you read over your second draft, check each sentence carefully for correctness.

- Have you written complete sentences?
- Does each sentence have a subject and a verb?
- Does the subject agree with the verb in each sentence?
- Have you used the correct verb tenses?
- Are there long sentences that should be divided?

Then check the mechanics of your paragraph.

■ Have you used correct punctuation?
■ Is your spelling correct?

Make these kinds of corrections as you write your third draft.

The Third Draft: Sentence Structure and Style

Read your third draft with these questions in mind:

■ Are your sentence openings varied, or do most of your sentences follow the subject-verb-complement pattern?
■ Do you use a mixture of sentence types: simple, compound, and complex?
■ Have you chosen words thoughtfully, maybe even tried to stretch your vocabulary?

The Final Draft

Now you are ready to write the final copy of your paragraph to hand in. Proofread your paper again very carefully. It might surprise you to find that you may want to make a few final changes or develop a particular idea more before you are completely satisfied.

ON YOUR OWN!

Choose one of the general topics in the list that follows. Narrow the topic down to a *very* small area that you can write about in detail in a single paragraph. For example, if you pick food as a general topic, you must narrow it down to a smaller topic such as junk food, fast food, Chinese (French, Italian, American) food, or health food.

Then, write a "perfect" paragraph, using all of the techniques you have learned in the last two chapters.

mixed marriages*	families
pollution	divorce
computers	AIDS
punk rock	artificial heart implants*
fashion	drugs
dating customs	suicide
space travel	food

---

mixed marriage: marriage between two people of different races, religions, or cultures
artificial heart implant: medical operation in which a man-made, mechanical heart is put in a person

Hints for Success

- Do the prewriting activities:
  1. Brainstorm.
  2. List your supporting points.
  3. Write a simple outline.
- Write a first draft from your outline.
- Revise your first draft: check the organization.
- Revise your second draft: check the grammar and mechanics.
- Revise your third draft: check the sentence structure and style.

chapter 6

Essay Organization

Model: Television—Harmful to Children

1   Over the past forty years, television sets have become standard pieces of equipment in most homes, and watching television has become a standard activity for most families. Children in our culture grow up watching television in the morning, in the afternoon, and often in the evening as well. Although there are many
5   excellent programs for children, many people feel that television may not be good for children. In fact, television may be a bad influence on children for three main reasons.

     First of all, some programs are not good for children to see. For example, there are many police stories on television. People are killed with guns, knives, and even
10 cars. Some children might think that these things could happen to them at any time. Therefore, they can become frightened. In addition, some youngsters might begin to think that violence is a normal part of life because they see it so often on television. They may begin to act out the violence they see and hurt themselves or their playmates.

15   Second, television can affect children's reading ability. Reading requires skills and brain processes that watching television does not. If children watch television too many hours each day, they don't practice the skills they need to learn how to read.

     Finally, television may affect children's schoolwork in other ways. If they spend
20 too much time watching television, they may get behind in their homework. Also, if they stay up to watch a late movie, they may fall asleep in class the next day. Consequently, they will not learn their lessons, and they could even fail in school.

     In conclusion, if children watch too much television or watch the wrong programs, their personalities can be harmed. Furthermore, their progress in school
25 can be affected. Therefore, parents should know what programs their children are watching. They should also turn off the television so that their children will study.

93

Questions on the Model

1. How many reasons does the author give for television's harmful effects on children? What are they?
2. Is violence a normal part of life?
3. Do you agree or disagree with the writer's point of view?

OVERVIEW OF ESSAY ORGANIZATION

In your college writing, you will be required to write essays (long compositions) and reports of more than one paragraph. In this chapter you will learn how to organize an essay.

An essay is made up of a group of paragraphs about one subject. A paragraph, as you learned in chapter 4, has three main parts: the topic sentence, the body, which is made up of supporting sentences, and the concluding sentence. The diagram that follows shows that an essay also has three main parts: the introduction, the body, and the conclusion.

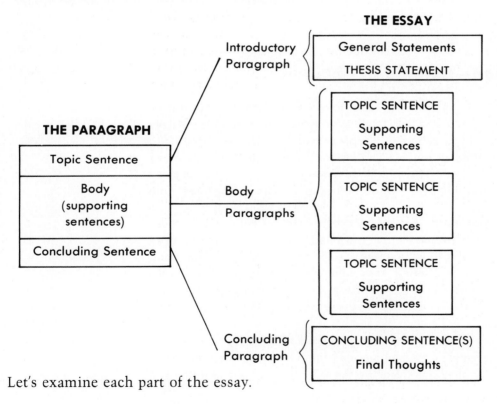

Let's examine each part of the essay.

THE INTRODUCTORY PARAGRAPH

The introduction is the first paragraph of the essay. It begins the essay and has two parts: general statements and the thesis statement.

General statements give the reader background information about the topic of the essay. They should be interesting enough to keep the reader's attention.

The **thesis statement** introduces the main idea of the essay.

- It states the main topic of the essay.
- It may list the subtopics of the main topic.
- It may also mention the method of organization.
- It is the last sentence of the introduction.

Reread the introductory paragraph of the model essay, "Television—Harmful to Children." Notice the general statements and the thesis statement.

- The first few statements present general background information on television and its place in our culture.
- The last sentence is the thesis statement. In the thesis statement, the writer states her opinion about the subject of too much television viewing for children: it's a bad influence. She also states that she will give reasons to support this opinion.

The number of general statements you write in an introduction will depend on how long your essay is. However, you should write at least two or three general statements in an introduction. The first sentence should be a very general comment about the subject. The second sentence should be less general, the third one should be even less general, and so on. The last general statement should be the least general of all.

After the last general statement, you write the thesis statement, which is the last sentence in the introduction. The thesis statement is the most specific statement of the introductory paragraph. It names the topic and the controlling idea(s) for the entire essay.

Notice that the structure of the model essay introduction, which moves from general statements to the specific thesis statement, resembles a funnel, wide at the top (beginning) and narrow at the bottom (end).

Over the past forty years, television sets have become standard pieces of equipment in most homes, and watching television has become a standard activity for most families. Children in our culture grow up watching television in the morning, in the afternoon, and often in the evening as well. Although there are many excellent programs for children, many people feel that television may not be good for children. In fact, television may be a bad influence on children for three main reasons.

PRACTICE: The Introductory Paragraph

Read the following introductory paragraphs, in each of which the sentences are in incorrect order. Rewrite each paragraph, beginning with the most general statement first. Then add each sentence in correct order, from the next most general to the least general. Finally, write the thesis statement last.

1. (1) Therefore, workaholics' lifestyles can affect their families, social lives, and health. (2) In addition, workaholics may not spend enough time in leisure activities. (3) Nowadays, many men and women work in law, accounting, real estate, and business. (4) These people are serious about becoming successful; they work long hours during the week and even on weekends, so they are called "workaholics."

_____

_____

_____

_____

_____

_____

_____

2. (1) Therefore, anyone who wants to drive must carry a driver's license. (2) It is divided into four steps: studying the traffic laws, taking the written test, learning to drive, and taking the driving test. (3) Getting a driver's license is a complicated process. (4) Driving a car is a necessity in today's busy society, and it is also a special privilege*.

_____

_____

_____

_____

_____

_____

_____

privilege: advantage that not everyone has

3. (1) During this period, children detach* themselves from their parents and become separate, independent individuals. (2) Teenagers express their separateness most vividly* in their choice of clothes, hairstyles, music, and vocabulary. (3) The teenage years between childhood and adulthood are a period of growth and separation.

_____

_____

_____

_____

_____

_____

_____

_____

_____

BODY PARAGRAPHS

The body of the essay is made up of one or more paragraphs. Each of these paragraphs has a topic sentence, supporting sentences, and sometimes a concluding sentence. Each of the body paragraphs supports the thesis statement.

Reread the body paragraphs of the model essay. The topic sentence of each paragraph states a reason why television is harmful to children. Then, each topic sentence is followed by several sentences that give facts or examples to support the topic sentence.

Thesis statement:
In fact, television may be a bad influence on children for three main reasons.

Topic sentences:
First of all, some programs are not good for them to see.
Second, television can affect children's reading ability.
Finally, television may affect children's schoolwork in other ways.

detach: separate, pull away
vividly: strongly

PRACTICE: Topic Sentences for Body Paragraphs

For the following thesis statements, write topic sentences for supporting body paragraphs. Follow the preceding example. Begin each topic sentence with a time order transition signal (*first, next*, etc.).

1. Young people who live at home have two advantages.

a. _____

b. _____

2. Owning a car is a necessity for several reasons.

a. _____

b. _____

c. _____

3. Women are superior to men in several ways.

a. _____

b. _____

c. _____

THE CONCLUDING PARAGRAPH

The conclusion is the last paragraph of the essay. It does three things.

■ It signals the end of the essay.
■ It summarizes the main points.
■ It leaves the reader with the writer's final thoughts on the subject.

Concluding Sentences

To signal the end of an essay, use a conclusion transition signal such as *in conclusion, in summary,* or *to summarize.* Then, either summarize the main points of the essay or rewrite the thesis statement in different words.

Thesis statement:
In fact, television may be a bad influence on children for three main reasons.

Conclusion:
In conclusion, if children watch too much television or watch the wrong programs, their personalities can be harmed. Furthermore, their progress in school can be affected.

PRACTICE: Concluding Sentences

A. Read the following thesis statements. Circle the letter of the most appropriate concluding sentence. Notice that each concluding sentence begins with a transition signal.

1. My greatest problem in learning English is oral communication.

   a. In conclusion, learning to read and write English is difficult.

   (b.) In conclusion, because I do not speak English enough, my listening and speaking skills have not improved.

   c. In conclusion, everyone should practice speaking English more.

2. Smoking is unhealthful because it can cause heart and lung disease; moreover, it is expensive.

   a. In brief, buying cigarettes is a bad idea.

   b. In conclusion, smoking affects your health, and it is also a waste of money.

   c. Therefore, smoking is a bad habit.

3. In my opinion, college grades are necessary because they motivate students to do their homework and to attend classes regularly.

   a. In conclusion, college grades are important.

   b. In conclusion, students should be graded for their own good.

   c. In conclusion, college grades are important because they cause students to be more serious and to try harder.

4. My major goals are getting a part-time job and mastering the use of the English language.

   a. In conclusion, if I do not reach my goals, I will be unhappy.

   b. In brief, finding a job and using English well are important to me.

   c. In summary, my major goals are getting a part-time job and mastering the use of the English language.

5. London has excellent bus and subway systems.

   a. In conclusion, the public transportation system in London provides reliable service at all times.

   b. In conclusion, taking a bus in London is convenient.

   c. In conclusion, taking public transportation is a good way to get around in London.

B. Read the following thesis statements. Write a concluding sentence based on the information in each thesis statement.

1. Drunk drivers are the greatest danger on our country's roads.

Therefore, *people shouldn't drink and drive.*

2. There are several disadvantages to owning a big car.

In conclusion, _____

_____

3. Smoking in restaurants should be banned* because it clouds the air, it smells bad, and it can ruin customers' appetites.

In conclusion, _____

_____

4. Eating in a restaurant is better than eating in a fast-food place because the atmosphere* is pleasant, the food is delicious, and the food is served to you.

_____

_____

Final Thoughts

In the second part of the concluding paragraph, after the concluding sentence(s), the writer gives his or her final thoughts on the subject of the essay. All the ideas in the body of the essay lead to the writer's final thoughts in the conclusion. For example, in the model essay, the writer makes two suggestions to parents as a final comment.

> Therefore, parents should know what programs their children are watching. They should also turn off the television so that their children will study.

Important! **Do not** add any new ideas in the conclusion because it is the end of your essay.

PRACTICE: Final Thoughts

A. Read the following conclusions. Circle the letter of the most appropriate final thought for each one. Notice the transition signals that introduce the writer's final thoughts.

---

banned: prohibited, forbidden   **atmosphere:** mood or feeling of a place

1. In conclusion, television provides many hours of good, free entertainment that the whole family can enjoy.

> **a.** However, television can also take over our lives if we do not know when to turn it off. Therefore, we must not watch television at the expense of other activities.

> **b.** However, violence on television can have a very negative effect on children because they cannot separate make-believe* from the real world.

> **c.** In fact, I like to watch about four hours of television every night.

2. In conclusion, smokers on the job make it uncomfortable for their co-workers*; furthermore, they are less productive on the job than nonsmokers.

> **a.** Therefore, smoking is bad for everyone's health.

> **b.** Therefore, smokers should smoke outside the workplace only.

> **c.** Therefore, if smokers want to get along with their co-workers and improve their work performance, they should stop smoking on the job.

3. In conclusion, it is no longer unusual to see men working as nurses, secretaries, and elementary school teachers.

> **a.** Indeed, there is less sexism* in the working world as men have proven themselves to be as capable as women.

> **b.** So, young boys should be encouraged to go into these careers.

> **c.** Therefore, women should become airline pilots, bridge construction workers, and symphony conductors.

B. Read the following concluding sentences. Write a final thought based on the information in each concluding sentence. Begin each of your final thoughts with a transition signal like *in my opinion* or *therefore*.

1. In conclusion, because a working mother has limited time, her husband should help with the children and housework as much as possible.

_____

2. In conclusion, people who like to get suntanned may get skin cancer.

_____

---

make-believe: something imagined or pretended   **co-workers:** people one works with
sexism: belief that men are better than women (or that women are better than men)

3. In conclusion, divorce produces many unhappy, lonely men and women, and it also affects their children.

MORE ABOUT THE WRITING PROCESS

As you learned in chapter 5, it is impossible to write a perfect paragraph on your first try; writing is an ongoing* *process.* Experienced writers constantly change words, sentences, or whole paragraphs. Beginning writers should do the same.

Use the following checklist when you revise your essays. Refer to it each time you prepare a final draft to hand in.

ESSAY CHECKLIST

Organization

Introduction:
  Do the general statements

  ■ give background information?
  ■ attract the reader's attention?

  Does the thesis statement

  ■ state a clearly focused main idea for the whole essay?

Body:
  Does each body paragraph have

  ■ a clearly stated topic sentence with a main (controlling) idea?
  ■ good development using sufficient supporting details and examples?
  ■ unity: does the paragraph support only one main idea?
  ■ coherence: does the paragraph follow a logical pattern and does the paragraph have transition words to connect ideas and to introduce a paragraph?

Conclusion:
  Does the conclusion

  ■ restate your thesis or summarize your main points?
  ■ give your final thoughts on the subject of your essay?

Grammar, Mechanics, and Sentence Structure

  ■ Are grammar, punctuation, and spelling correct?
  ■ Have you used a variety of sentence openings and sentence types?

ongoing: continuing

PRACTICE: Revising the Essay

A. The following essay needs to be revised. It has some problems in each of its paragraphs. Refer to the Essay Checklist as you study the essay paragraph by paragraph.

Work with a partner or with a small group. One person in each group should write down the problems in each part of the essay as they are being discussed.

After the group discussion is completed, join in a class discussion to compare your findings with those of the other groups.

Heavy Traffic

1   The traffic problem is growing in most big cities. There are many overcrowded streets and freeways. Because there are too many cars and other vehicles. There are not enough parking facilities in the busy downtowns areas. However, the heavy traffic problem can be solved in three ways.

5   More rapid transit systems should be build between the cities and suburbs. Then, people who lives in the suburbs and works in the cities can get to their destinations* quick and safely. By using rapid transit systems, commuters* will leave their cars at home. This will reduce the number of cars on the freeways. And the streets in the busy downtown areas. Many people like to

10   shop in the department stores in big cities. In Japan the metropolitan areas have excellent railway lines for commuting within the cities. There are also dependable subway systems to connect large city like Tokyo and Osaka.

Car pools are a good way to ease the heavy traffic during the commuter rush hours. A car pool is an arrangement by a group of car owners to take turns

15   driving their car to work and other places. For example. If several people live near one another in the same suburb and work in a big city. Like Boston, Manhattan, or Los Angeles, they can form a car pool. They can take turns driving to the city and back. With more people using car pools. There will be fewer traffic jams and accidents. Public transportation systems within the cities

20   must be improved. People who live in large cities should take buses and streetcars to go downtown. If they leave their cars at home. They can avoid the commuter rush. They can get to their destinations and return home much more quickly.

In conclusion, car pools are necessary.

B. Rewrite the essay above. Correct the organization, paragraphing, sentence structure, and grammar as necessary.

---

destination: the place where someone or something is going
commuter: a person who travels regularly between two points

chapter 7

Business Letters

Model: Letter of Application

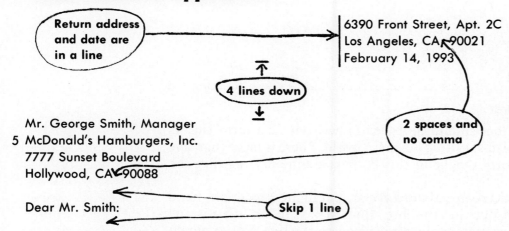

Return address and date are in a line

6390 Front Street, Apt. 2C
Los Angeles, CA 90021
February 14, 1993

4 lines down

2 spaces and no comma

Mr. George Smith, Manager
5 McDonald's Hamburgers, Inc.
7777 Sunset Boulevard
Hollywood, CA 90088

Dear Mr. Smith:

Skip 1 line

I would like to apply for the position of night manager in your restaurant on
10 Sunset Boulevard.

Skip 1 line between paragraphs

My work experience includes one year as a kitchen helper at Sam's Chinese
Restaurant, one and one-half years as a gas station attendant, and various*
temporary jobs during school vacations. During the past three months at Sam's,
I have supervised five other part-time kitchen workers. I also cook occasionally.* At
15 the gas station, I learned how to deal with* customers, handle large amounts of
money, and work under pressure* during rush hour.* Currently, I am a student
at the University of California, majoring in business management.

---

various: several, different
occasionally: sometimes
pressure: force, necessity

rush hour: very busy period of time
to deal with: to take care of

I believe that the skills I have acquired* in these two jobs qualify* me for your position. May I call you next week to schedule an interview? Thank you for your
20 time and attention.

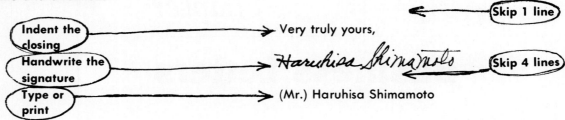

Indent the closing → Very truly yours, ← **Skip 1 line**

Handwrite the signature → *Haruhisa Shimamoto* ← **Skip 4 lines**

Type or print → (Mr.) Haruhisa Shimamoto

Questions on the Model

1. What is the main purpose of this letter? In which paragraph and in which sentence is the main purpose stated?
2. In which paragraph does the writer give additional information about himself?
3. What is the purpose of the last sentence in the letter?

ORGANIZATION

Business Letter Form

All business letters should be typed or written in a form that is standard* in the English-speaking business world. There is more than one standard form; the form taught in this book is commonly* used in the United States.

The **writer's address** and the **date** are put in the upper right-hand corner of the page. Notice that the three lines make a block—that is, the first words in each line start at the same place on the line. Notice where periods and commas are used—and also where they are **not** used (before a ZIP code). Follow this form *exactly*.

6390 Front Street, Apt. 2C
Los Angeles, CA 90021
February 14, 1988

---

acquired: gotten
qualify: have the knowledge, skill, and ability to do something

standard: customary, usual
commonly: generally, usually

ABBREVIATIONS COMMONLY USED IN ADDRESSES

Apt.	Apartment
Ave.	Avenue
Blvd.	Boulevard
Co.	Company
c/o	in care of
Dr.	Drive
Inc.	Incorporated
Ltd.	Limited
No.	Number
P.O.	Post Office
Rd.	Road
St.	Street (also Saint, as in St. Mary's College)

The **receiver's name** and **address** is placed on the left. It should start at least four lines down from the date line. Again, it makes a block—the first words in each line start at the same place on the line. Again, pay attention to the punctuation and follow the example *exactly.*

Mr. George Smith, Manager
McDonald's Hamburgers, Inc.
7777 Sunset Boulevard
Hollywood, CA 90088

COMMONLY USED TITLES

Mr.	married or unmarried man
Ms.	married or unmarried woman
Mrs.	married woman
Miss	unmarried woman

NOTE: Because *Miss* is not an abbreviation, there is no period after it. The other titles listed are abbreviations.

The **greeting** is placed two lines down from the last line of the receiver's address. In other words, skip one line before you write the greeting. The standard greeting is *Dear (title) (name):.* If you do not know the person's name, you may write *Dear Sir/Madam:.* Put a colon [:] after the greeting.

Dear Mr. Brown:
Dear Professor Kassler:
Dear Ms. Sims:
Dear Sir/Madam:

The **body** of the letter may be one paragraph or many. Skip a line between paragraphs, and indent the first line of each new paragraph.

The **closing** is placed two lines below the body of the letter and a little to the right of center. Capitalize only the first word and put a comma after the last word. Here are some customary closings for business letters.

COMMONLY USED CLOSINGS

Sincerely,
Sincerely yours,
Very truly yours,
Respectfully,
Cordially, (only if you know the person you are writing to)

Your name is typed or printed four lines below the closing. Notice that the closing and your name make a box—the first words start at the same place on the line. You write your signature in handwriting between the closing and your typed or printed name. You should always write your signature in black or dark blue ink.

Two special notes about names:

- In English, we write our first names first and our family names last. You should follow this custom although it may seem strange to you. For example, a person from Korea whose name is Choi Byuong should always write his name Byuong Choi in English.
- It is usually not polite to give your own title. However, if your name is unfamiliar to native English-speakers, you need to indicate whether you are a man or a woman by putting *Mr., Ms., Mrs.,* or *Miss* in parentheses in front of your name. Putting it in parentheses is a polite way of telling the receiver of your letter whether to write, for example, "Dear *Ms.* Shimamoto" or "Dear *Mr.* Shimamoto."

If you are sending something in the same envelope with the letter, it is customary to type the word *Enclosure* (or its abbreviation *Encl.*) at the left below your name.

On the **envelope**, write the receiver's name and address just the same as you wrote it in the letter. In the upper left-hand corner of the envelope, write your full name and complete address. The envelope for the model letter should look like this:

```
Haruhisa Shimamoto
6390 Front St., Apt. 2C                          ┌──────┐
Los Angeles, CA  90021                           │ STAMP│
                                                 └──────┘


          Mr. George Smith, Manager
          McDonald's Hamburgers, Inc.
          7777 Sunset Boulevard
          Hollywood, CA  90088
```

ONE FINAL NOTE: You should type all business letters if possible. If it is not possible, you may *neatly* write a business letter on unlined white 8½″ × 11″ paper (standard-size business stationery). You should use black or dark blue ink. Keep approximately the same spacing as in the model, and leave at least one-inch margins on all sides. Finally, *print* your name below your signature clearly.

Business Letter Content: One-Paragraph Letters

Good business letters in English are short and to the point. They should contain only enough information to accomplish* their purpose and no more. It is not customary to comment on the weather or on anything personal. In general, the shorter a business letter is, the better it is.

For example, for a simple business matter, one sentence is enough.

Dear Sir/Madam:

Please send your most recent catalog and price list to me at the address given above.

Sincerely,

Here is another example of a short but good business letter, this one an order for a book:

Dear Sir/Madam:

Please send me, at the address given above, one copy of *Write It Right* by William Penn. Enclosed is my check for $13.27.

Sincerely,

PRACTICE: One-Paragraph Letters

On five pieces of plain white paper, address letters from yourself to the following people or institutions.* Then, choose *one* of the five and write a short letter requesting whatever is named in parentheses. Also, address an envelope correctly with both your and the receiver's addresses. Punctuate and capitalize carefully.

1. professor john knight/ chairman/ english department/ university of texas/ post office box 600/ dallas/ texas/ 20010 (Ask him for a list of English courses that are taught during the summer semester.)

2. mary k. lamb/ president/ cabbage patch computer company/ incorporated/ 5470 north riverside drive/ chicago/ illinois/ 50033 (Ask her for a list of software companies that sell software for your computer. You have a Cabbage Patch computer, model no. 007.)

accomplish: finish successfully   **institution:** organization (business company, school, etc.)

3. office of admissions/ graduate school of business/ stanford university/ palo alto/ california/ 94305 (Ask for a catalog of courses for the Graduate School of Business.)

4. the head of your English program or school (Ask for a copy of your grades.)

5. the editor of your school newspaper (Ask for a copy of the latest edition of the newspaper.)

Business Letter Content: Three-Paragraph Letters

You have already learned one rule about business letters: keep them short and to the point.* Now let's learn and practice how to write business letters that require more than one paragraph.

Many business letters that you, as a student, will need to write will have more than one paragraph. You may have to write a letter of application (for a job or to a school) or a letter asking for something—information about colleges, for example. A letter can be divided into paragraphs just as a composition can. The parts of a letter are like the parts of a composition. In a three-paragraph letter, this would be the plan:

Paragraph Number	Name of Part	Purpose
1	Introduction	State the purpose of the letter (your main idea)
2	Body	Give supporting information
3	Conclusion	Ask for or announce action; say thanks

Look back at the model letter of application on page 105 and review the "Questions on the Model" on page 106.

1. What is the main purpose of the letter? Where is Mr. Shimamoto's reason for writing stated?
2. What is the purpose of the middle paragraph? Is all of this information necessary? Is any of it unimportant?
3. Does Mr. Shimamoto ask for or announce action? What is that action? How does he end the letter?

In the first paragraph of his letter, Mr. Shimamoto states his reason for writing: he wants to apply for a job at McDonald's. Not only does he say that he wants to apply for a job, but he also mentions the specific job: night manager. Furthermore, if he had learned about the job through a newspaper advertisement, he should have said so: "I would like to apply for the job of night manager at your restaurant on Sunset Boulevard. I saw the advertisement for the position in today's *Los Angeles Times.*" In short,*

---

to the point: concerning the most important part of a topic
in short: in summary

say why you are writing right at the beginning of your letter and be as specific as possible.

In the middle paragraph, Mr. Shimamoto gives additional information about himself: he tells about past jobs he has had that are relevant* to this job. This is the place where he tries to "sell himself"—to convince* Mr. Smith that he is qualified. Notice that he does not give unnecessary information; Mr. Smith does not need to know the color of his eyes, for example, or whether or not he can play the piano. If he has any other strong points, he should mention them here—but only those points that are important to the job at McDonald's.

In the last paragraph of his letter, Mr. Shimamoto announces what he will do: he will call Mr. Smith next week to make an appointment for an interview. Sometimes it is more appropriate to tell the receiver what you want him or her to do. Again, be very specific. Finally, say thanks in the last sentence.

In summary, this division into paragraphs is typical for a three-paragraph business letter:

  I. Tell why you are writing.
 II. Give additional necessary information.
III. Say what you will do or what you want the reader to do. Say thanks.

PRACTICE: Business Letter Content

A. Analyze the organization of the letter on page 118 (Dictocomp) by answering these questions:

  1. How many paragraphs does the letter have? How many paragraphs are in the body of the letter? Why?

  2. What is the purpose of the first paragraph?

  3. What information does the second paragraph give or ask for? Why is this information necessary?

  4. What information does the third paragraph give or ask for?

  5. Does the conclusion paragraph ask for action or announce action?

B. Indicate by number (1, 2, or 3) in which paragraph of a three-paragraph business letter the following sentences belong. Be able to tell whether each sentence states the purpose of the letter, gives additional information, announces action, asks for action, or expresses thanks.

———— **1.** Kindly send the catalog to me at the following address:
     (Miss) Anna Phanutaiwat
     c/o U. C. Leong
     576 Rana Road
     Bangkok, Thailand

relevant: connected with, important
convince: make someone believe

____ **2.** I am currently* a senior at the University of Colorado, majoring in economics.

____ **3.** Thank you in advance for your assistance.

____ **4.** I am interested in applying for admission to your graduate program in international banking and finance.

____ **5.** With sincere appreciation for your prompt reply, . . .

____ **6.** I would appreciate your sending the information as soon as possible.

____ **7.** I am writing to request information about your "Work/Study in Spain" program.

____ **8.** Please send the application form via airmail to me at the address given above.

____ **9.** I speak Spanish and English fluently, and I can read and understand some French.

____ **10.** I will call your office next Wednesday to make an appointment for an interview.

GRAMMAR AND MECHANICS

Present Perfect Tense

The **present perfect tense** links the past with the present. Use it when an action began in the past and is still continuing in the present. Use it also when the action still affects the present, or when it is important in some way to the present in the mind of the speaker.

> I have lived at home with my parents all my life.
> (I still live there.)
> I have never seen a shooting star. (But I still might see one.)
> How long have they been married? (They are still married.)

Also, the time words *since* and *yet* require the present perfect tense.

> My two uncles haven't spoken to each other since 1954. (They are still not speaking to each other.)
> Have you finished your homework?
> No, I haven't finished it yet. (. . . but I will finish it.)

---

currently: now

RULES FOR PRESENT PERFECT VERB FORMS

Present perfect verb forms are made by combining *has* or *have* with the past participle of the verb:

I	have worked	we	have worked
you	have worked	you	have worked
he/she/it	has worked	they	have worked

The past participle of most verbs is formed by adding *-ed* to the simple form.

- Regular verbs:

has/have walked	(*walk* + *ed*)
has/have played	(*play* + *ed*)
has/have answered	(*answer* + *ed*)

- Regular verbs with spelling changes:

has/have scared	(*scare* + *ed*—drop the *e*)
has/have cried	(*cry* + *ed*—change the *y* to *i*)

- Irregular verbs: The past participle forms of many verbs are irregular, so they must be memorized. You will find a list of irregular verbs in grammar books and dictionaries.

has/have said	(present perfect of *say*)
has/have spent	(present perfect of *spend*)
has/have written	(present perfect of *write*)
has/have done	(present perfect of *do*)

PRACTICE: Present Perfect Tense

A. Fill in the blanks in the following composition with the present perfect form of the verb given in parentheses.

1   It is Thanksgiving morning at the Smiths' house. Mrs. Smith

(be) *has been* in the kitchen since sunrise. She *has*

already (begin) *begun* to cook the Thanksgiving meal,

which the family will eat about four o'clock in the afternoon. The Smiths

5 (invite) _____ all of their close relatives to spend the day

with them. The Smith family (celebrate) _____ Thanksgiving

together for the past twenty-five years although sometimes they

(eat) _____ dinner at another family member's house.

These are the things that Mrs. Smith _____ already

10 (do) _____: she (bake) _____ four

pies, she (mix) _____ the dressing for the turkey

(a mixture of bread cubes, onions, celery, and spices), she

(fill) _____ the inside of the turkey with the dressing,

and she (put) _____ the turkey in the oven to cook.

15   These are the things that Mrs. Smith (not do) _____

yet: she (not prepare) _____ the vegetables, and she

(not make) _____ the salad yet. Also, she (not have)

_____ time to set the table.

It is now three o'clock in the afternoon. It is almost time to eat. Mrs. Smith

20 and her children _____ almost (finish) _____ their

work. They (set) _____ the table, they (make) _____

the salad, and they (cook) _____ the vegetables. They

_____ just (go) _____ to their rooms to change into their good clothes.

25   Most of their relatives _____ already (arrive) _____.

Only Uncle Bob and Aunt Margaret and their family (not come) _____ yet. As soon as they arrive, the family (all twenty-one of them) will sit down at the table and enjoy the meal they (wait) _____ all day for!

B. Imagine that you are the owner of a store or restaurant in your area. You need to hire some students to work part-time. Write down eight to ten questions to ask each applicant. The questions should be about the applicants' education and work experience. Write them in the present perfect tense if it is appropriate*.

    Have you ever had a job before?
    Where have you worked?

Now, trade questions with a classmate, and write answers to each other's questions.

C. Imagine that you are a well-known television news reporter who interviews famous people all over the world. Think of a famous person about whom you would like to know more, and write five questions in the present perfect tense to ask him or her. Your famous person may be living or dead, and the questions may be serious or humorous.

    (for Queen Elizabeth II of England)
    Have you ever washed dishes?
    How many years have you been a queen?
    (for Yuri Gargarin, first man in space)
    Have you ever been afraid of the dark?

Now, exchange papers with a classmate, and write answers to each other's questions.

Present Perfect vs. Simple Past Tense

The **simple past tense** is the verb form used for an action that began in the past and was completed in the past. The present perfect is used for an action that began in the past but is still happening or is still influencing the present.

---

appropriate: correct, suitable

Simple Past	Present Perfect
I <u>lived</u> in Hawaii for three years. (I don't live there now.)	I <u>have lived</u> in Hawaii for three years. (I moved there three years ago, and I am still living there.)
She <u>lived</u> a happy life. (She is dead.)	She <u>has lived</u> a happy life. (She is still living.)
They <u>got</u> married in 1980. (Their wedding was in 1980.)	They <u>have been</u> married since 1980. (They are still married. Remember that *since* requires the present perfect.)
They <u>were</u> married for a year. (They aren't married now.)	They <u>have been</u> married for a year. (They are still married.)

PRACTICE: Present Perfect vs. Simple Past Tense

A. In the following sentences, choose either simple past or the present perfect form of the verb in parentheses, and write it in the blank.

1. Van Ng and his family (leave) _____ Vietnam in 1978.

2. They (wait) _____ in a refugee camp in Thailand for

   six months until they (receive) _____ permission to enter the United States.

3. Now Van and his family are living in Texas. They (live)

   _____ there since 1985.

4. Before that, they (live) _____ in Minnesota, but it

   (be) _____ too cold there, so they (move)

   _____.

5. Van's father (not find) _____ a job in Texas yet.

6. When they were in Minnesota, he (work) _____ on a dairy farm.

7. Van and his brothers (study) _____ English at a special school for refugees in Minnesota.

8. Since last year, however, they (attend) _____ the local school with American children.

9. Van's older brother is the only one who doesn't go to school because

   he (already graduate) _____ from high school. He

   (graduate) _____ two years ago.

10. A big problem for the Ng family when they first (come) _____

to America (be) _____ the food; they (not like)

_____ it.

11. At first, Mrs. Ng (cook) _____ only Vietnamese food
for her family.

12. When they (move) _____ to Texas, however, she

(become) _____ friends with a Mexican neighbor.

13. Her new friend (teach) _____ her how to prepare

spicy Mexican food, and *chili con carne* (be) _____ a
family favorite ever since then.

14. However, they (not learn) _____ to enjoy American
hamburgers yet.

15. Although the Ngs (live) _____ in the United

States for more than six years, they (not give up) _____
hope of returning to their country.

B. Write two or three paragraphs about yourself. In one paragraph, write
about your education, both in the past and now. When did you start
school? How many schools have you attended? When did you attend each
school? What classes have you studied? How long have you been / were
you in high school? How long have you attended your present school?
How many years ago did you finish elementary school? What did you
learn?

You might write sentences like the following. (Be careful to use
simple past and present perfect appropriately.)

> I started school when I was five years old. I have been a student
> for seventeen years now...

In another paragraph, write about any jobs or work experience you
have had in the past.

> Last year, I worked for my father in his business.

In another paragraph, write about what you have always liked or
hated to do. Write three or four sentences to explain why.

> I have always loved to eat. The kitchen has always been my
> favorite room in the house...
>
> I have always hated to do homework. When our teacher gave
> us...

DICTOCOMP

The following letter is an example of another common kind of business letter: a letter asking for something. In this letter, the writer, a student, is asking for information. Write the letter as your teacher dictates it to you.

1
                                                    10 Downing Street
                                                    Boston, MA 20302
                                                    March 15, 1993

Mr. Thomas E. Brown, Director of Admissions
5 Sagebrush College
P. O. Box 212
Brownsville, TX 20222

Dear Mr. Brown:

   I am interested in applying for admission to your college next fall.

10   I am a graduate of St. Mary's High School in Singapore and have spent the past two semesters studying English. My most recent TOEFL score was 517. I plan to major in computer science.

   I would like some information about your college. First, I would like to know what your TOEFL requirement is. Second, please tell me how many foreign students your college has. Third, I am interested in finding out whether your college has other
15 students from Singapore. Finally, I need to know if I can live in a dormitory on campus, or if I have to rent an apartment off campus.

   Please send application forms and the other information to me at the address above. Thank you.

20   Very truly yours,

                                                  Osei Tsai

                                                  (Miss) Osei Tsai

SENTENCE STRUCTURE

Complex Sentences with Noun Clauses

As you remember, a complex sentence is made of one independent clause and one or more dependent clauses. One kind of dependent clause is called a **noun clause.** It is called a noun clause because it acts like a noun: it can be a subject or, more often, an object.

Look at these two sentences:

   Please tell me the price.
   Please tell me how much it costs.

In the first sentence, the direct object of the verb *tell* is a noun: *the price.* In the second sentence, the direct object is a noun clause: *how much it costs.*

There are three kinds of noun clauses:

- *that* noun clauses, which are made from statements
- *wh-* word noun clauses, which are made from *wh-* questions
- *if/whether* noun clauses, which are made from yes/no questions

THAT NOUN CLAUSES

That noun clauses are made from statements. (**Statements** are sentences that end with a period.) To change a statement into a dependent noun clause, put the word *that* in front of it. Then, to make a complete complex sentence, attach it to an independent clause such as "I would like to know...," "Please tell me...," "She doesn't remember...," or "Is it true...?"

Statement:	The moon is made of green cheese.
Noun clause:	...that the moon is made of green cheese.
Independent clause:	People used to believe (something).
Complete sentence:	People used to believe that the moon is made of green cheese.

(The word *that* may sometimes be omitted: People used to believe the moon is made of green cheese.)

PRACTICE: *That* Noun Clauses

A. Combine each independent clause from the list on the left with the statement that follows it on the right to make a complex sentence containing a *that* noun clause. Write the sentences in the form of a paragraph.

Independent Clauses	Statements
Yesterday Anna discovered.	She had become a millionairess.
She didn't think.	She would ever be so lucky.
The lawyer told her.	Her Aunt Beulah had willed* Anna all her money and property.
Now she knew, of course.	She would never have to work again.
She didn't want the town to find out.	She had a lot of money.
How would it feel to learn?	You were a rich person.

willed: given away

Yesterday Anna discovered that she had become a millionairess.

_____

_____

_____

_____

_____

_____

_____

B. Write five complex sentences of your own that contain dependent *that* noun clauses. If you wish, write humorous, even ridiculous* *that* clauses.

> It is not true that my uncle wears a toupee.*
>
> Do you believe that UFO's* exist?

WH- WORD NOUN CLAUSES

Wh- word noun clauses are dependent clauses formed from questions beginning with the words *who, what, when, where, why,* and *how.* To change a *wh-* question into a dependent noun clause, change the word order back to normal statement word order (subject before verb). Then attach it to an independent clause to make a complete complex sentence. Watch what happens to the verb.

Wh- question:	Where **did** he **buy** his new car?
Noun clause:	. . . where he **bought** his new car.
Independent clause:	No one knows.
Complete sentence:	No one knows where he bought his new car.

Notice that *did buy* becomes *bought.* Do not use the auxiliary (helping) verbs *do, does,* or *did* in a noun clause. Here's another example:

Wh- question:	How much **does** a round-trip ticket from Hong Kong to Paris **cost**?
Noun clause:	. . . how much a round-trip ticket from Hong Kong to Paris **costs**.
Independent clause:	We were surprised at (something).
Complete sentence:	We were surprised at how much a round-trip ticket from Hong Kong to Paris costs.

Again, *does cost* becomes *costs.*

---

ridiculous: silly, nonsensical
toupee: false hair

UFO: unidentified
flying object

Now notice what sometimes happens when the *wh-* word is *who* or *what*:

Wh- question:	Who wants to go skiing next weekend?
Complete sentence:	The director needs to know who wants to go skiing next weekend.

As you can see, the word order does not change when the *wh-* word is *who*.

There is one case, however, when the word order changes: when the verb is a form of *be* and the word *who* or *what* and the noun after the *be* verb refer to the same person or thing.

Wh- question:	Who is the richest woman in the world?
Noun clause:	. . . who the richest woman in the world is.
Independent clause:	I don't know.
Complete sentence:	I don't know who the richest woman in the world is.

In this example, *who* and *the richest woman in the world* refer to the same person. Notice how the word order changes: the verb comes at the end.

Here is an example using *what*:

Wh- question:	What is your name?
Noun clause:	. . . what your name is.
Independent clause:	I can't remember.
Complete sentence:	I can't remember what your name is.

In this example, *what* and *your name* refer to the same thing. Therefore, the verb comes at the end.

PRACTICE: *Wh-* Word Noun Clauses

A. Change the following *wh-* questions into dependent noun clauses and attach each one to any appropriate independent clause from the list to make a complete complex sentence. Remember not to use *do, does,* or *did* as helping verbs in the dependent noun clause.

How much did her new car cost?
It's rude* to ask how much her new car cost.
What did you do last night?
I don't want to tell you what I did last night.

---

rude: not polite

Independent Clauses	Wh- Questions
It's rude to ask.	Why do they have so much homework every night?
I don't want to tell you.	How many girlfriends does he have?
Jeanne promised not to tell.	Who is that handsome man?
Do you know?	How old is she?
The police want to find out.	Where did they go last weekend?
The prisoner wouldn't say.	What is your telephone number?
His wife doesn't know.	When is the teacher's birthday?
She doesn't care.	Who stole the painting?

B. This exercise is for additional oral practice. Student 1 asks a *wh-* question such as "How old is [name of student 3]?" Student 2 says to student 3, "[Name of student 1] wants to know how old you are." Student 3 can either answer the question or avoid answering it by saying something such as "It's rude to ask how old I am," or "I don't want to tell you how old I am."

IF/WHETHER NOUN CLAUSES

If/whether noun clauses are made from yes/no questions. To change a yes/no question into a noun clause, add either *if* or *whether* at the beginning, change the word order back to normal statement word order (subject before verb). Then, attach it to an independent clause to make a complete complex sentence.

Yes/no question:	Is it going to rain today?
Noun clause:	. . . whether it is going to rain today. . . . if it is going to rain today.
Independent clause:	The weatherman doesn't know.
Complete sentence:	The weatherman doesn't know whether it is going to rain today.
(or)	The weatherman doesn't know if it is going to rain today.

NOTE: *If* and *whether* mean the same. If you use *whether*, you may add the words *or not* immediately after the word *whether* or at the end of the clause—but you don't have to. If you use the word *if*, you may add *or not* **only** at the end of the clause.

The weatherman doesn't know whether it is going to rain today.
The weatherman doesn't know whether or not it is going to rain today.
The weatherman doesn't know whether it is going to rain today or not.
The weatherman doesn't know if it is going to rain today.
The weatherman doesn't know if it is going to rain today or not.

PRACTICE: *If/Whether* Noun Clauses

A. An amnesia* victim has just walked into a New York City police station. He can't remember who he is, where he is from, or how he got there. A police officer is questioning him. Each time the officer asks him a question, he answers, "I don't know . . ." or "I can't remember . . ." or "I can't tell you . . .". Of course, change each question into a noun clause.

1. Do you live in New York?

I don't know if I live in New York.

2. Are you married?

3. Do you have any family?

4. Did you come here in a taxi or did you walk?

5. Do you have a driver's license?

6. Have you ever had amnesia before?

7. Were you in an accident recently?

8. Can you read and write English?

9. Have you been in this police station before?

10. Did you eat breakfast this morning at home?

amnesia: total loss of memory

B. For additional oral practice, ask and *avoid answering* yes/no questions in pairs. One student asks a yes/no question, and the other student avoids answering by saying, "I don't know whether . . . ," "I can't remember if . . . ," or "I don't want to tell you . . . ."

You may also practice *if/whether* noun clauses by the same kind of exercise as you did with *wh-* word noun clauses. Student 1 asks a yes/no question about student 3, and student 2 repeats it with the words "_____ (name of student 1) wants to know whether (if) . . . ." Student 3 avoids answering the question.

C. Find and underline all of the noun clauses in the letter on page 118 (Dictocomp). Then, rewrite them as questions.

D. Pretend that you are writing a letter to a school to which you want to apply. You have several questions about the school.

Write five *wh-* questions, and then change them into *wh-* noun clauses and attach each one to an appropriate independent clause.

Do the same with five yes/no questions.

> When does the next school term start?
> Would you please tell me when the next school term starts?

> Can students live in dormitories?
> I would like to know if students can live in dormitories.

Here are some suggestions for independent clauses to use in a business letter. You and your classmates can probably think of others.

> I would like to know (something).
> Would you please tell me?
> I am interested in finding out (something).

ON YOUR OWN!

Choose either of the following assignments and write a letter that has at least three paragraphs. Plan your letter before you write it by making a brief outline first. Have your teacher check it. Then, write the letter, using the correct form and punctuation you have learned in this chapter. Use only plain white paper and dark blue or black ink. Type your letter if possible. Finally, address an envelope for your letter.

A. Your younger brother (or sister) wants to come to your school to learn English. Write a letter to an administrator or a teacher in your school or college and ask him or her to send application forms and information to your brother (or sister). Give enough information about your brother (or sister) so that the school administrator can send appropriate information. Include two or three noun clause questions in your letter.

B. Choose one of the following want ads for jobs that appeared in the newspaper. Write a letter of application for the job.

Ad #1: Bookstore clerk. Should enjoy reading. Should be friendly and have good clerical skills. Must be able to work four days per week, including weekends. Please write to Stinson Beach Books, P. O. Box 428, Stinson Beach, CA 94970.

Ad #2: Dishwasher. No experience required, but must have a neat appearance. Must be willing to work at night. Four hours per day, six days per week. Opportunity to learn food preparation. Write to Lau Yee Chow Restaurant, 1234 Petticoat Lane, London, England. Please send a recent photo with your letter.

Ad #3: Babysitter needed afternoons, 3 or 4 days per week and occasional evenings. Two children, ages 6 and 8. Must be at least 16 years old. Write to Dr. and Mrs. Benjamin Spock, 65 Waimea Street, Honolulu, HI 99989.

Ad #4: Dog walker. I need someone to take my pet dog for a walk every afternoon. Hours flexible. Salary negotiable. Must love dogs. Write to Mrs. George Fields, 118 South 64th Street, Washington, DC 00111.

Prewriting Activities

Work together with a partner or with a small group to plan your letter. Answer the following questions. Then make a rough outline with the information you have.

- Address:
    - Whom will you write to?
    - Get the correct address.
- Paragraph 1:
    - What should you say in the first paragraph?
    - Does the person you are writing to know you, or should you explain who you are?
- Paragraph 2:
    - What additional information should you give?
- Paragraph 3:
    - What questions can you ask?
    - What action should be taken?
    - What else belongs in this paragraph?

chapter 8

Classification

Model: Holidays

1   Holidays around the world can be classified on the basis of their origins*. Almost all of them began as pagan* festivals, anniversaries of important historical or political events, or religious days.

The first group of holidays began as pagan festivals. In many cultures, people
5 celebrate the end of winter and the beginning of spring. The beginning of spring was often the beginning of the new year. A very clear example of a modern holiday with pagan origins is *No Rooz*, Iranian New Year. It is celebrated on the first day of spring with bonfires and special foods. There is also a special table that displays seven objects whose names begin with the letter *s*. Another example of a modern
10 holiday with pagan origins is the American Halloween, which is on October 31st. On Halloween night, children dress up in costumes and go from house to house to get candy. They say "trick or treat," which means, "If you don't give me candy, I will play a trick on you." The children often dress up as witches*, ghosts*, or black cats. People also carve frightening faces in pumpkins* and put candles inside them at
15 night. All of these customs started hundreds of years ago in Ireland and England. Ancient people there celebrated the end of the farming season by lighting bonfires. They also dressed up as ghosts to frighten away bad spirits, which they believed came back to earth on that night.

The second group of holidays celebrates important historical or political
20 events. National independence days, such as July 1st in Canada and July 4th in the United States, are in this category. An important person in history is Christopher Columbus, who discovered the New World in 1492. Columbus Day is celebrated in both North and South America. Furthermore, almost all countries celebrate the birthday of their greatest leader. Finally, various patriotic holidays belong in this
25 group. In the United States, people who died in wars are honored on Memorial Day,

---

origin: beginning
pagan: not religious
witch: old woman possessed
 by evil spirits

ghost: spirit of a dead person
pumpkin: large, round, orange-colored
 vegetable that grows on a vine

and Guy Fawkes' Day is celebrated in England because of the capture of an English traitor*.

30 The third category of holidays includes all of those holidays that have religious origins. Moslems, for example, celebrate *Eid*, which comes at the end of a month of fasting. Buddhists in Japan have a flower festival and parade on April 8, which is Buddha's birthday. The Jewish religion has many important celebrations such as Rosh Hashanah, Passover, and Hanukkah. Christians celebrate the birth of Jesus at Christmas and his resurrection* at Easter. Valentine's Day was originally the birthday of a Christian religious man whose name was Saint Valentine. In many 35 countries, it is a popular day when friends and lovers exchange cards and gifts.

In conclusion, the word *holiday* is a combination of the words *holy* and *day*, but as we have seen, not all holidays are religious. They may also be pagan or patriotic in origin.

Questions on the Model

1. What basis does the writer use to divide holidays into groups? What are the groups?
2. What are examples of holidays with pagan origins?
3. Why do people in North and South America celebrate Columbus Day?
4. What are some examples of patriotic holidays that the writer mentions?
5. What is Saint Valentine's Day?

ORGANIZATION

Classification

When you write an essay on a large topic, you must divide it into paragraphs. One method of dividing a large topic is to separate parts of it that have something in common into groups. This method is **classification.** In the model essay, for example, the basis for classifying the different holidays is their origin—religious, patriotic, or pagan.

To further understand how classification works, study how the following list of sports has been divided. The basis for classification is the time of year each sport is played.

List of sports, unclassified:

baseball	ice hockey	swimming
bobsledding	ice-skating	table tennis
bowling	jogging	tennis
fishing	mountain climbing	volleyball
golf	scuba diving	waterskiing
gymnastics	skiing	windsurfing
hiking	soccer	

---

traitor: spy   **resurrection:** rising from the dead

List of sports, classified according to season of the year in which each is played:

I. Summer sports

A. Baseball	F . Scuba diving
B . Fishing	G. Soccer
C. Golf	H. Tennis
D. Hiking	I . Waterskiing
E . Mountain climbing	J . Windsurfing

II. Winter sports
   A. Bobsledding
   B . Ice hockey
   C. Ice-skating
   D. Skiing

III. Year-round sports

A. Bowling	D. Swimming
B . Gymnastics	E . Table tennis
C. Jogging	F . Volleyball

PRACTICE: Classification

Study the following outlines and decide what bases were used to classify the same list of sports. (Notice that bobsledding can be in either group when the first basis for classification is used.) Fill in the blanks.

A. Basis for classification: _____

    I. _____

A. Bobsledding	H. Jogging
B . Bowling	I . Mountain climbing
C. Fishing	J . Scuba diving
D. Golf	K . Skiing
E . Gymnastics	L . Swimming
F . Hiking	M. Waterskiing
G. Ice-skating	N. Windsurfing

    II. _____

A. Baseball
B . Bobsledding
C. Ice hockey
D. Soccer
E . Table tennis
F . Tennis
G. Volleyball

B. Basis for classification: _____

    I. _____

        A. Baseball
        B. Bowling
        C. Golf
        D. Soccer
        E. Table tennis
        F. Tennis
        G. Volleyball

    II. _____

        A. _____

            1. Fishing
            2. Scuba diving
            3. Swimming
            4. Windsurfing
            5. Waterskiing

        B. _____

            1. Bobsledding
            2. Ice Hockey
            3. Ice-skating
            4. Skiing

    III. _____

        A. Hiking
        B. Jogging
        C. Mountain climbing

Can you and your classmates think of other ways to classify the list of sports?

Outlining

While you have been learning about classification, you have also been learning how to outline. **Outlining** is a way to help you organize your ideas. It helps you plan your essay before you begin to write it.

A simple outline looks like this:

    Topic sentence
    A. Supporting detail
    B. Supporting detail
    C. Supporting detail

A more complex outline looks like this:

   I. Topic sentence
     A. Main idea
       1. Supporting detail
       2. Supporting detail
     B. Main idea
       1. Supporting detail
       2. Supporting detail
       3. Supporting detail
     C. Main idea
       Supporting detail
  II. Topic sentence
     A. Main idea
       1. Supporting detail
       2. Supporting detail
       3. Supporting detail
     B. Main idea
       Supporting detail
     C. Main idea
       Supporting detail

Notice these points:

- The topic sentence of each paragraph is given a Roman numeral (I, II, III, IV, V, VI, VII, VIII, IX, X, etc.).
- Each main idea is given a capital letter (A, B, C, D, E, F, etc.). If there are no main ideas, but only supporting details, then they are given letters as in the first outline.
- Each supporting detail is given an Arabic number (1, 2, 3, 4, 5, etc.).
- Indent each time you move from a Roman numeral to a capital letter to an Arabic number. Indenting makes it easy to see that you are moving from big to small, from main ideas to specific details.
- There should be at least two items in a group in order to give them letters and numbers. In the preceding outline, only one supporting detail is given under I. C. and II. B. C.; therefore, no number is given. However, the single supporting detail is indented in line with the other supporting details that are numbered.

PRACTICE: Classification/Outlining

A. Review the model essay about holidays and complete the outline that follows.

Holidays

 I. Introduction

II. The first group of holidays began as pagan festivals.

A. Spring festivals

_____ (example)

B. _____

_____ (example)

III. The second group of holidays celebrate important historical or political events.

A. _____

   1. July 1st – Canada

   2. _____

B. Birthdays

   Greatest leaders

C. Other patriotic holidays

   1. _____

   2. _____

IV. _____

A. _____

B. _____

C. Jewish holidays

   1. _____

   2. _____

   3. _____

D. Christian holidays

   1. _____

   2. _____

   3. Valentine's Day

V. Conclusion

B. You should now be ready to classify a topic on your own. Classify the items in any two of the following lists.

First, decide on the basis for your classification. There may be more than one possible basis for classifying the items. Your basis may be different from those of your classmates. Then, make an outline.

1. Shopping in a Supermarket

aspirin	cookies
bread	eggs
apples	steak
carrots	ground meat
oranges	roast beef
milk	shampoo
cheese	tomatoes
lettuce	fish
potatoes	cake
vitamins	toothpaste
pie	breakfast rolls

2. Leisure-Time Activities

watching a movie	visiting a museum
disco dancing	attending a concert
bowling	attending a lecture
watching TV/video	hiking
reading	listening to music at home
playing chess	listening to music at a
shopping	friend's house
skateboarding	playing arcade games

3. Furniture

stove	sofa
floor lamp	table lamps
dining table and	microwave oven
six chairs	upholstered chair
refrigerator	footstool
piano	flower vase
coffee table	alarm clock
end tables	Oriental rug
chandelier	chest of drawers
nightstand	coffee maker
twin beds	buffet
stereo system	
television	

4. Famous Disasters in History

Disaster	Place	Date	Deaths
Chemical factory leak	Bhopal, India	1985	2,000
Volcano eruption/tsunami	Krakatoa, Indonesia	1883	36,000
Earthquake	Tangshan, China	1976	800,000
Sinking of ship *Titanic*	North Atlantic	1912	1,500
Airplane collision	Canary Islands	1977	600
Earthquake	Mexico City, Mexico	1985	5,000
Flood	Huang He River, China	1931	3,700,000
Earthquake	Iran	1978	25,000
Hindenburg crash	New Jersey, USA	1937	36
Cyclone	Bangladesh	1970	300,000
Cyclone	Bangladesh	1985	10,000
Windstorms	Bangladesh	1965	57,000
Dam break	Italy	1985	200
Nuclear power plant fire	Chernobyl, USSR	1986	3
Space shuttle *Challenger* crash	Florida, USA	1986	7

5. Problems of a Large City

There are more than 70,000 factory chimneys in the city.
The average person has only 70 square feet of living space.
Over 15,000,000 people live within the city limits.
About 200 traffic injuries happen every day.
Ten thousand new cars are registered each month in the city.
Traffic control policemen need to breathe oxygen.
There were 400,000 applicants for 54 public housing apartments last
   year.
On the average, rent takes 65 percent of a family's income.
Forty tons of soot* fall yearly on every square mile.
To purchase a car, people must prove they have a parking place that
   is not on the street.
The cost of food has tripled in the last 10 years.

C. At the 1938 World's Fair in New York, a time capsule* was put in the ground. It contained items that were examples of American life in the 1930s: a telephone, a wristwatch, a package of cigarettes, a can opener, a piece of coal, a woman's hat, and samples of cloth, seeds, and plastics. Of course, there were newspapers, magazines, and a motion picture film. The capsule is supposed to be opened in the year 6939, five thousand years after the New York World's Fair closed.

Suppose you and your classmates were given the job of selecting items for a time capsule this year, to be opened after five thousand years. As a class or in small groups, make a list of objects that you think are good examples of life in your country today. Next, classify them into categories

---

soot: black powder produced by smoke
time capsule: container that holds objects of a current society and that is buried so that it can be studied by a future society

such as technology, agriculture, entertainment, education, fashion, or any other categories you and your classmates choose. Then, hold a class discussion to decide which objects are the best examples of contemporary* culture. Because the size of the time capsule is limited to five square meters, you can only put two items from each category in it. Finally, make an outline of your results.

Using Examples for Support

Whenever you make a statement that is not an obvious truth, you need to prove it. One way to prove that a statement is true is to support it with examples.

Suppose you wrote this thesis sentence:

> Manhattan is a wonderful place to visit if you are planning a trip to the United States.

If your readers have never been to Manhattan, you will have to convince them that Manhattan is worth visiting. To convince them, you could describe some of Manhattan's tourist attractions. These would be examples.

> I. Manhattan has many tourist attractions. (topic sentence)
>   A. Greenwich Village (example)
>   B. Statue of Liberty (example)
>   C. Central Park (example)
>   D. Chinatown (example)
>   E. Metropolitan Museum (example)

In another paragraph, you could write about the variety of fine restaurants in Manhattan.

> II. Furthermore, there is an unlimited selection of fine restaurants in Manhattan (topic sentence)
>   A. French—Les Pyrenees (example)
>   B. Italian—La Scala (example)
>   C. Chinese—The Four Seasons (example)
>   D. Japanese—Benihana of Tokyo (example)
>   E. Thai—Bangkok 54 (example)

You could also write about the excellent shopping, hotels, or nearby tourist attractions such as Times Square and the United Nations. You would write a separate paragraph for each topic and give specific examples of shops, hotels, and nearby attractions.

Examples don't have to be proper nouns, of course. They can also be statements of fact. For instance, you would have to use facts to prove statements such as the following:

> I. Women are safer drivers than men. (topic sentence)

These two sentences describe examples of women's safer driving:

> A. Women receive fewer speeding tickets. (example)
> B. Women have fewer accidents. (example)

---

contemporary: current

PRACTICE: Examples

A. Find all of the examples in the model essay on page 127 and underline them.

B. Individually or in groups, think of examples to support the following statements (whether you agree with them or not).

Group A—Use single nouns as examples.

  I. Some of the world's strongest leaders have been women.
    A. Indira Ghandi
    B.
    C.
    D. (add more if you can)

 II. Rock stars don't stay popular very long.
    A. Michael Jackson
    B.
    C. (add more if you can)

III. Some sports require extraordinary* courage.
    A.
    B.
    C. (add more if you can)

Group B—Use complete sentences as supporting examples.

  I. Young people today are under more stress than their parents were.
    A. They face more competition* in school.
    B.
    C. (add more if you can)

 II. Drug abuse* is not the only problem among today's youth.
    A.
    B.
    C.

INTRODUCING EXAMPLES

You should introduce examples in your paragraphs by using one of the following phrases:

For example, _____(sentence)_____.

For instance, _____(sentence)_____.

---

extraordinary: exceptional   **abuse:** improper use
competition: the act of trying to win something against someone else

One
Another
An } example of (noun phrase) is (noun phrase).
A second
A third

_____ (noun phrase) _____ is an example of

_____ (noun phrase or clause) _____ .

... such as _____ (noun phrase) _____ ...

For example and *for instance* are interchangeable and can come at the beginning, in the middle, or at the end of a sentence. Notice the commas in these examples:

> For example, teenagers today have to study harder in school.
> **or**
> Teenagers today, for example, have to study harder in school.
> **or**
> Teenagers today have to study harder in school, for instance.
> One example of a nearby tourist attraction is Lake Tahoe, where one can look at beautiful scenery or gamble* in busy casinos*.
> Michael Jackson is an example of a rock musician whose star rose and fell within a year or two.
> New York's excellent Chinese restaurants, such as The Four Seasons, are famous around the world.

C. Find and circle the words and phrases that introduce examples in the model essay on pages 127–128.

FREEWRITING

Write complete paragraphs from two of the outlines you just completed in Practice B. Choose one from each group so that you practice using both proper nouns and sentences as examples. You may use the topic sentence given to begin your paragraph.

Use the phrases listed on page 136 and above to introduce your examples. Try to use each phrase at least once.

---

gamble: play cards or other games to win money
casino: building where games for money are played

GRAMMAR AND MECHANICS

Restrictive and Nonrestrictive Appositives

Appositives are nouns or noun phrases that refer to the same person or thing as a preceding noun in a sentence. Appositives can be **restrictive** (necessary) or **nonrestrictive** (unnecessary).

Consider this sentence:

My friend Tim got married last week.

In this sentence, *Tim* is an appositive because *Tim* and *my friend* are the same person. *Tim* is a restrictive (necessary) appositive because it is necessary to identify which friend got married. If we omit the word *Tim*, we don't know which friend got married.

On the other hand, consider this sentence:

Tim, my friend, got married last week.

In this sentence, the appositive is *my friend.* It is nonrestrictive (unnecessary) because the name *Tim* already identifies the person who got married. If we omit *my friend*, we still know who got married. The fact that he is the writer's friend is not necessary to identify him. It is merely extra information.

If there is only one of an item that is referred to in a sentence, it is unnecessary to identify it further, so appositives of one-of-a-kind items are always nonrestrictive. For example, Earth has only one moon, so any appositive of *the moon* in a sentence would be nonrestrictive. Similarly, adjectives such as *tallest, strongest, oldest, most interesting* automatically make the following noun one of a kind.

My son Andrew looks just like me. (Because there is more than one son, *Andrew* is necessary to identify which one the writer means. *Andrew* is a restrictive appositive.)

My youngest son, Thomas, looks just like his father. (Because there is only one youngest son, *Thomas* is not necessary here. It is a nonrestrictive appositive.)

COMMA RULE

Commas are used to separate nonrestrictive (unnecessary) appositives from the rest of the sentence. Commas are not used with restrictive (necessary) appositives.

PRACTICE: Commas with Restrictive and Nonrestrictive Appositives

Underline the appositive in each of the following sentences. Then decide whether it is necessary or unnecessary and write *necessary* or *unnecessary* in the parentheses following each sentence. Finally, add commas to separate an unnecessary appositive from the rest of the sentence.

1. The planet <u>Pluto</u> is over two and a half billion miles from Earth. (_____*necessary*_____)

2. Pluto, <u>the most distant planet from Earth,</u> is over two and a half billion miles away. (_____*unnecessary*_____)

3. Venus the closest planet to Earth is only twenty-five million miles away. (_____)

4. The largest planet in the universe Jupiter is eleven times larger than Earth. (_____)

5. The moon is Earth's only satellite, but the planet Saturn has at least twenty-two satellites. (_____)

6. Astronomers scientists who study the stars believe that there is another planet in our solar system. (_____)

7. Neptune one of the farthest planets from Earth will be photographed in 1989 by the space probe Voyager II. (This sentence has two appositives.) (_____) (_____)

8. Andrew the Queen of England's second son married Sarah Ferguson a commoner in 1986. (This sentence has two appositives.)

   (_____) (_____)

9. The Queen's son Charles will become king of England one day.

   (_____)

10. The terrible disease AIDS has killed thousands of people.

    (_____)

11. Governments are spending millions of dollars to combat AIDS a fatal illness. (_____)

12. The world was shocked when movie star Rock Hudson died of AIDS.

    (_____)

Restrictive and Nonrestrictive Adjective Clauses

Adjective clauses are clauses that modify* nouns. They begin with the words *who, whom, which, whose, where, when,* and sometimes *that.* You will learn how to write them in the next section. In this section, you will learn when to use commas with them.

Adjective clauses can be restrictive or nonrestrictive, just as appositives can. Use the same comma rule:

■ restrictive (necessary): no commas
■ nonrestrictive (unnecessary): use commas to separate the adjective clause from the rest of the sentence.

Look at this sentence:

The planet that is nearest to Earth is Mars.

In this sentence, the clause "that is nearest to Earth" is an adjective clause that modifies the noun *planet.* It is necessary to identify which planet the writer is discussing, so the clause is restrictive and commas are not used. *That* always introduces a restrictive clause.

Now consider this sentence:

Water once covered Mars, which is Earth's nearest neighbor.

In this sentence, the clause "which is Earth's nearest neighbor" is an adjective clause that modifies the noun *Mars.* The clause is unnecessary to identify Mars; it merely gives extra information about it. Therefore, commas are used before and after the clause. *Which, who, whom, when,* or *where* introduce a nonrestrictive clause.

Here are two examples of sentences that contain adjective clauses beginning with the word *where.* What nouns do each of the clauses modify?

The Sea of Tranquillity is the place where man first landed on the moon. (necessary, no commas)
The Sea of Tranquillity, where man first landed on the moon, is a large, smooth crater.* (unnecessary, so commas are used)

PRACTICE: Commas with Restrictive and Nonrestrictive Adjective Clauses

Underline the adjective clauses in the following sentences and draw an arrow to the noun each one modifies. Then, decide whether each one is necessary or unnecessary, and write the words *necessary* or *unnecessary* in the parentheses following each sentence. Finally, add commas if they are needed.

1. Millions of people watched television on the day when man first

landed on the moon. (*necessary*)

---

modify: describe   **crater:** a huge bowl-shaped hole

2. Millions of people watched television on July 20, 1969, when man first landed on the moon. (*unnecessary*)

3. The animal that can run faster than any other animal in the world is the cheetah. (_____)

4. Cheetahs which can run twice as fast as humans reach speeds of seventy miles per hour. (_____)

5. The deadly black mamba snake which lives in Africa can move at a speed of twenty miles per hour. (_____)

6. A person whom a black mamba bites will die if he or she doesn't receive medical treatment. (_____)

7. Most poisonous snakes are found in areas where the climate is warm.

(_____)

8. The saw-scaled or carpet viper snake whose bite causes severe bleeding and fever kills more people than any other snake.

(_____)

9. A mollusk in a beautiful seashell that is found in the South Pacific and Indian oceans can kill people. (_____)

10. Three fish that are deadly are the octopus, the stingray, and the stonefish. (_____)

11. Most snakebites happen during warm weather when snakes are active, not in winter when they hibernate*. (This sentence contains two adjective clauses.) (_____) (_____)

12. I think I'll move to either Hawaii or Ireland where there are no snakes at all. (_____)

---

hibernate: go into a long sleep in winter

DICTOCOMP

Write the following paragraphs as your teacher dictates them to you.

1   April Fool's Day, which is celebrated on the first day of April in some countries, is always a lot of fun. It is a day when people play tricks on one another. People who don't remember what day it is may have a lot of surprises. My twin brother, who loves to play tricks on other people all year long, spends weeks thinking up new
5   jokes to play on this special day.

No one knows when April Fool's Day began, but some people believe it started in India long ago. There, people celebrate a spring holiday that is called *Holi*. People fill bamboo pipes with colored powders and blow them at other people. Anyone who is outside may come home at the end of the day looking like a
10 rainbow*!

SENTENCE STRUCTURE

Complex Sentences with Adjective Clauses

In this section, you will learn how to write complex sentences with adjective clauses. You may remember from the preceding* section that adjective clauses are clauses that modify nouns.

Look at this sentence:

Easter, which is a Christian holiday, is named for a pagan goddess.

The clause "which is a Christian holiday" is an adjective clause that modifies the noun *Easter.*

Adjective clauses begin with one of the following words, which are called **relative pronouns:** *who, whom, which, whose* (+ noun), *where,* or *when.* In restrictive clauses **only,** you use the word *that* in place of *which.* The correct relative pronoun to use depends on whether the rela-

---

rainbow: half-circle of many colors that may appear in the sky after rain
preceding: the one before

tive pronoun is the subject or the object of its clause, whether it shows possession, and whether it refers to people, things, places, or times.

Since an adjective clause is a dependent clause, it cannot stand alone. It must be joined to an independent clause to make a complete complex sentence. When you join them, put the adjective clause after the noun it modifies in the independent clause. Finally, add commas if the adjective clause is nonrestrictive.

SUBJECT PATTERN ADJECTIVE CLAUSES

When a relative pronoun is the subject of an adjective clause, the clause is a **subject pattern adjective clause.** You form subject pattern adjective clauses by changing the subject of a sentence to *who* (for people), *which* (for animals and things), or *that* (for people, animals, or things in restrictive clauses).

Look at these two sentences:

Easter is a Christian holiday.
Albert Einstein was one of the world's most famous physicists.

We can turn the first sentence into an adjective clause by changing *Easter* to *which.* We can do the same to the second sentence by changing *Albert Einstein* to *who.* We can add each of these clauses to an independent clause to make a complex sentence as follows:

Independent clause:	Easter is named for a pagan goddess.
Dependent adjective clause:	*which* ~~Easter~~ is a Christian holiday.
Complex sentence:	Easter, which is a Christian holiday, is named for a pagan goddess.
Independent clause:	Albert Einstein failed his university entrance examination.
Dependent adjective clause:	*who* ~~Albert Einstein~~ was one of the world's most famous physicists.
Complex sentence:	Albert Einstein, who was one of the world's most famous physicists, failed his university entrance examination.

PRACTICE: Subject Pattern Adjective Clauses

A. Make an adjective clause from the sentence in parentheses in each of the following pairs. Write it in the space provided to make a complete complex sentence. Add commas if they are needed.

1. Many religions have rules about food *that were developed for health reasons* . (The rules were developed for health reasons.)

2. Judaism _____
has very strict rules about food. (Judaism is the oldest major religion
in the world.)

3. Christians _____
do not eat certain foods during the six weeks before Easter.
(Some Christians practice fasting*.)

4. People _____
cannot eat beef. (People practice the Hindu religion.)

5. Moslems and Jews cannot eat pork _____

_____. (Pork is considered unclean.)

6. Moslems cannot eat or drink at all in the daytime during *Ramadan*

_____. (*Rama-
dan* is a holy month of fasting.)

B. Combine the sentences in each of the following pairs by making one of
them an adjective clause and joining it to the other sentence. Be careful to
put the clause immediately after the noun it modifies. Add commas if
they are needed.

1. Three of the world's major religions were started by men. The men
were teachers.

Three of the world's major religions were started by men who

were teachers.

2. Gautama Siddhartha was born about five hundred years before Jesus.
Gautama Siddhartha started Buddhism.

_____

_____

3. Christianity was started by Jesus Christ. Jesus Christ was born about
five hundred years before Mohammed.

_____

_____

---

fasting: act of eating no food or only certain foods for a period of time

4. A religion is monotheistic. A religion has one God.

_____

_____

5. The Hindu and Shinto religions are polytheistic. The Hindu and Shinto religions have many gods.

_____

_____

OBJECT PATTERN ADJECTIVE CLAUSES

When the relative pronoun is an object in an adjective clause, the clause is called an **object pattern adjective clause.** You form object pattern adjective clauses by changing any object in a sentence to *whom* (for people), *which* (for animals and things), or *that* (for animals or things in restrictive clauses). It is also possible to omit the relative pronoun in the object pattern.

The object can be a direct object, indirect object, or object of a preposition.

> I read a <u>newspaper story</u> recently. (direct object)
> The story told about a <u>Japanese kimono</u>*. (object of preposition)
> The kimono brought great misfortune to <u>its owners</u>. (indirect object)

We can turn these sentences into adjective clauses by changing the objects to *that* and putting these relative pronouns before the subjects of the sentences. We can add each of these clauses to an independent clause to make a complete complex sentence as follows:

Independent clause:	I was very interested in a newspaper story.
Dependent adjective clause:	*that* ↙ I read a ~~newspaper story~~ recently.
Complex sentence:	I was very interested in a newspaper story that I read recently.
Independent clause:	A Japanese kimono belonged to three different girls.
Dependent adjective clause:	*that* ↙ The story told about a ~~Japanese kimono~~.
Complex sentence:	A Japanese kimono that the story told about belonged to three different girls.

---

kimono: long Japanese garment

PRACTICE: Object Pattern Adjective Clauses

A. Make an adjective clause from the sentence in parentheses in each of the following pairs. Write it in the space provided to make a complete complex sentence. Add commas if they are needed.

1. A story *that I read in a newspaper* told about a deadly* Japanese kimono. (I read the story in a newspaper.)

2. The kimono _____ may have started a great fire in Tokyo in 1657. (Three different girls had owned the kimono.)

3. The fire _____ killed 100,000 people. (The kimono started the fire.)

4. Each girl _____ died before she had a chance to wear it. (The kimono belonged to each girl.)

5. A priest _____ knew what to do. (The parents of the third girl told a priest about the kimono.)

6. The priest decided to burn the kimono _____

_____. (People thought the kimono was unlucky.)

While the priest was burning the kimono, a wind started to blow, causing the fire to spread. Three-fourths of Tokyo was destroyed, and 100,000 people died.

B. Combine the sentences in each of the following pairs by making one of the sentences an adjective clause and joining it to the other sentence. Be careful to put the adjective clause immediately after the noun it modifies. Add commas if they are needed.

1. The book *Strange but True Stories* tells about water monsters*. Many people don't believe in monsters.

   The book Strange but True Stories tells about water monsters,

   which many people don't believe in.

2. One of the world's most famous water monsters is the Loch Ness monster in Scotland. The book tells about a water monster.

   _____

   _____

deadly: causing death   **monster:** strangely-shaped, frightening animal

3. The Loch Ness monster lives in a lake. People have named the monster Nessie.

_____

_____

4. A scientist believes that Nessie is real. The Academy of Applied Science sent a scientist to find and photograph Nessie.

_____

_____

5. The photographs show a large sea snake with flippers*. The scientist took photographs.

_____

_____

POSSESSIVE ADJECTIVE CLAUSES

You form **possessive adjective clauses** by changing a possessive word to _whose_. The possessive word can be a possessive pronoun (_my, his, her, its, our, your, their_), or a possessive noun (_Mary's, my friend's, the children's, the girls'_).

Look at this sentence:

His real birthday is unknown.

We can turn this sentence into a possessive adjective clause by changing _his_ to _whose_. When we join it to an independent clause, the result is a complex sentence.

Independent clause:	On December 25, Christians celebrate the birth of Jesus Christ.
Dependent adjective clause:	~~His~~ _whose_ real birthday is unknown.
Complex sentence:	On December 25, Christians celebrate the birth of Jesus Christ, whose real birthday is unknown.

flipper: "leg" of a sea animal such as a seal

PRACTICE: Possessive Adjective Clauses

A. Make a possessive adjective clause from the sentence in parentheses in each of the following pairs. Write it in the space provided to make a complete sentence. Add commas if they are needed.

1. A widow is a woman *whose husband is dead* _____.
(A woman's husband is dead.)

2. The first president of the United States was George Washington
_____. (George Washington's birthday is a national holiday.)

3. Any horse _____
must be killed. (His leg is broken.)

4. A person _____
will probably die. (The person's temperature goes higher than 107 degrees Fahrenheit.)

5. However, Bryden Lando, a young boy _____
_____ after he fell into a frozen river, didn't die. (His temperature dropped to 70 degrees Fahrenheit.)

6. Halley's comet _____
will not return for seventy-five years. (Its last appearance was in 1986.)

B. Combine the sentences in each of the following pairs by making one of them a possessive adjective clause and joining it to the other sentence. Be careful to put the clause immediately after the noun it modifies. Add commas if they are needed.

1. UFO's (unidentified flying objects) are fascinating. Most scientists don't believe in their existence.

   UFO's, whose existence most scientists don't believe in, are

   fascinating.

2. The story of a young Brazilian farmer was in all the newspapers ten years ago. His experience is especially interesting.

   _____

   _____

3. The young man believes that he was taken aboard a UFO. The young man's name is Antonio Vargas.

_____

_____

4. He said some space creatures had kidnapped him. He later drew the space creatures' pictures.

_____

_____

5. The space creatures examined him. He could not understand their language.

_____

_____

6. He said a woman was attracted to him. Her appearance was very human-like.

_____

_____

TIME AND PLACE ADJECTIVE CLAUSES

You form place and time adjective clauses by changing a place expression to *where* or a time to *when* and placing the relative pronoun in front of the subject. Remember that adjective clauses, like adjectives, modify (describe) nouns.

Look at this sentence:

Santa Claus lives at the North Pole.

We can make it into an adjective clause by changing *at the North Pole* to *where.* Then we can join this clause to an independent clause to make a complex sentence.

Independent clause: It is always cold at the North Pole.

Dependent adjective clause: Santa Claus lives ~~at the North Pole.~~ *where*

Complex sentence: It is always cold at the North Pole, where Santa Claus lives.

In this sentence, "where Santa Claus lives" is an adjective clause because it modifies the noun *North Pole.*

Here is an example with an adjective clause beginning with *when*:

Independent clause:	The second most important holiday in the United States is Thanksgiving Day.
Dependent adjective clause:	Families spend the whole day preparing and eating a special meal ~~on Thanksgiving Day~~. *when*
Complex sentence:	The second most important holiday in the United States is Thanksgiving Day, when families spend the whole day preparing and eating a special meal.

PRACTICE: Time and Place Adjective Clauses

Make an adjective clause beginning with either *when* or *where* from the sentence in parentheses in each of the following pairs. Write it in the space provided to make a complete complex sentence. Add commas if they are needed.

1. Do you remember the year *when Russia sent the first person into space?* (Russia sent the first person into space in that year.)

2. The International Date Line, *where each day begins,* _____ is not a straight line, but a zigzag*. (Each day begins at the International Date Line.)

3. On Thanksgiving _____ people travel great distances to be with their families. (Americans eat the same food that the Pilgrims* ate on Thanksgiving.)

4. On November 1st and 2nd _____ the spirits of dead relatives are welcomed back to Earth for a visit. (People in Mexico celebrate the Days of the Dead on November 1st and 2nd.)

5. On the island of Haiti _____ people can return from death. They can walk, but not talk. (People believe in black magic* in Haiti.)

---

zigzag: series of short lines shaped like the letter "z"
Pilgrim: member of one of the first European groups who came to America. The Pilgrims were religious people who arrived in Plymouth, Massachusetts, in 1620.
black magic: magic with a bad purpose

6. Every American over the age of forty remembers what she or he was doing on the day _____.
(President John F. Kennedy was assassinated* on the day.)

7. Can you name two islands _____?
(There are no snakes on those islands.)

PRACTICE: Adjective Clauses

A. Find and underline all of the adjective clauses in the model composition, "Holidays," on pages 127 and 128.

B. Write sentences with adjective clauses on your own. Define each of the following words with a sentence that contains an adjective clause. Use the words in parentheses to build your definition. Look up the words you don't know in a dictionary.

1. fortune teller (a person): *A fortune teller is a person who can see into the future.*

2. October 31 (the day): *October 31 is the day when American children celebrate Halloween.*

3. travel agent (a person): _____

4. bank (a place): _____

5. unicorn (an animal): _____

6. orphan (a child—use a possessive adjective clause): _____

7. mah-jongg (a game): _____

8. January 1st (the day): _____

---

assassinate: murder by surprise attack

9. Puerto Rico (a place): _____

_____

10. Valentine's Day (a day): _____

_____

11. fork (a utensil): _____

_____

12. chopsticks (utensils): _____

_____

13. (Think up some words of your own to define.) _____

_____

14. _____

_____

_____

15. _____

_____

16. _____

_____

17. _____

_____

PRACTICE: Sentence Combining

In the following composition, combine the sentences in brackets [ ] to make compound or complex sentences. Look for opportunities to make complex sentences containing adjective clauses.

A True News Story

1   [Police in Brookfield, Connecticut, a small town in the United States, recently arrested a man. The man was possibly the world's stupidest robber.] [The man was picked up by a passing motorist. The man was hitchhiking.] [The motorist was hit in the face by the man. The motorist was robbed by the man.]
5 The hitchhiker stole the motorist's wallet.

[The robber got home. He discovered that the wallet was empty. He had stolen the wallet.] Also, his own wallet was missing. [He had left his wallet

in the motorist's car. It contained seventy dollars.] [The hitchhiker called the
motorist on the telephone. He offered to exchange wallets.] [The motorist
10 agreed to meet him at a certain corner in the town. There was a police station
at that corner.] [The robber arrived at the meeting place. The police arrested
him.]

ON YOUR OWN!

Choose one of the following topics and write an essay at least five
paragraphs long, using classification as a means of organizing your ideas.

> Holidays in My Country
> My City (Country)—A Great Place to Visit!
> Pollution
> Favorite Leisure-Time Activities
> Types of Teachers (movies, books, friends, television programs,
> television commercials, automobiles, music, jewelry, students,
> crimes, criminals, hobbies, etc.)
> Problems of Students in My Country
> Roles of Family Members (your father, your mother, your
> grandparents, and you)

Hints for Success

- Do the prewriting activities:
  1. Brainstorm for ideas and choose a basis for classification.
  2. Make an outline.
- Write your first draft, and check it against the essay checklist on
  page 102.
  1. Use examples to support each main idea.
  2. Use a combination of sentence types.

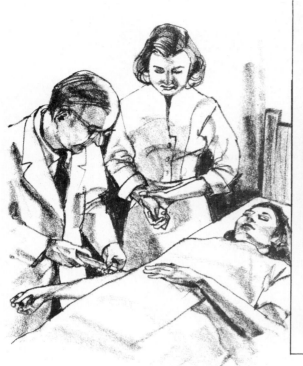
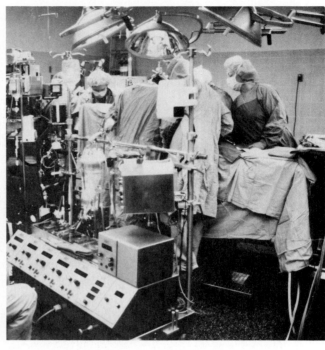
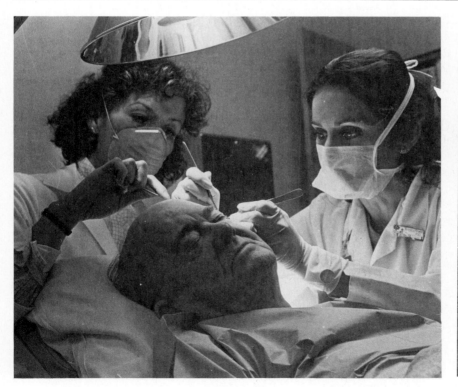

chapter 9

Persuasion

Model: The Right to Die

1   A difficult problem that is facing society today is euthanasia, another word for mercy killing. Thousands of young people are in comas* because of accidents, and old people are terminally* ill because of incurable* diseases. They are all kept alive in artificial ways. They have no chance to recover completely, but the American
5 legal system does not allow doctors to end their lives. However, terminally ill patients should be allowed to die for several reasons.

    The first and most important reason is that the patients have no chance of recovery. They can never lead normal lives and must be kept alive by life-support machines*. They may need a machine to breathe and a feeding tube to take in
10 food. They are more dead than alive and will never get better. For example, in 1975, Karen Quinlan became unconscious after she swallowed some drugs and drank alcohol. She was kept alive by machines. Her parents knew that her body and brain would never be normal. Therefore, they asked the court to allow their daughter to die. The judge agreed, and Karen's breathing machine was turned off.
15 She was able to breathe on her own, but she died nine years later in June of 1985.

    The second reason is that medical costs are very high. The cost of a hospital room can be as much as five hundred dollars per day and even more. The costs of medicines and medical tests are also high. The family of the patient is responsible for these expenses. Consequently, they would be a terrible financial burden* for
20 them for a long time.

    The third reason is that the family suffers. The nurses can only give the terminally ill patient minimum care. The family must spend time to care for the special needs of their loved one. They should talk, touch, and hold the patient even

---

coma: unconscious state (cannot see, hear, or speak)
terminally: will end in death
incurable: cannot be cured, cannot be made healthy again
life-support machines: machines that keep people alive
burden: problem

155

though he or she may be in a coma. For example, Karen Quinlan's parents visited
25 her every day even though she was unable to speak or to see. Also, it is very difficult
to watch a loved one in a coma because his or her condition doesn't improve.

In conclusion, because terminally ill patients have no chance to live normal
lives, they should be allowed to die with dignity*. Therefore, the family should have
the right to ask doctors to turn off the life-support machines or to stop further
30 medical treatment.

Questions on the Model

1. What is euthanasia?
2. Who was Karen Quinlan?
3. What would be a terrible financial burden for the family?
4. How does the family suffer?
5. What is the topic sentence of each of the three body paragraphs?
6. What words begin each of the topic sentences?
7. Do you agree with the writer's argument? Why or why not?

ORGANIZATION

Persuasive Essays

When you have an opinion and try to persuade someone (your
listener or reader) to accept your opinion, you are arguing *for* or *against*
something. For example, in an everyday situation, you may try to persuade
a friend to have lunch or dinner at an Italian restaurant instead of at a
Chinese one. Or, you may try to convince someone to buy a red sports car
instead of a blue sports car. In a college composition or speech class, the
instructor may make an assignment in which you must argue *for* (support)
or *against* (oppose) the use of nuclear energy to produce electricity. In the
business world, if you sell Triumph computers, you, of course, want your
customers to buy your products instead of a competitor's. Therefore, you
will try to convince your customers that your product and models are the
best on the market. In any situation, whether you are speaking or writing,
when you want to win someone over to your way of thinking, you are
using **persuasion.**

Using Reasons to Support an Opinion

An **opinion** is what a person thinks about a subject. In the model
composition, the writer says that people who cannot recover from their
illnesses should have the right to die. That is the writer's opinion. She
supports her opinion with several reasons.

Paragraph 2: The patients have no chance for recovery.
Paragraph 3: Medical costs are very high.
Paragraph 4: The family suffers.

dignity: state or quality of high regard, respect, worth

Reread the second, third, and fourth paragraphs of the model composition. You will see that the writer has supported each of her reasons with facts and/or examples.

A **fact** is a true statement that can be proven. When you give your opinion about a subject, you want your reader to agree with you. So, you must give reasons for your opinion. One of the ways to support your reasons is to give facts. Read the following example:

Thesis Statement:
Alcoholic beverages should be banned from college campuses for two reasons.

According to the controlling idea of the thesis statement, the writer is going to discuss two reasons why alcoholic beverages should not be allowed on college campuses.

Topic Sentence 1:
The first reason is that drinking can cause academic failure.

The topic sentence in question form is, "How can drinking cause academic failure?" The answers to that question will supply the specific details to explain or support the topic sentence.

Main Supporting Ideas:
—Unable to concentrate
—Miss classes, fail exams, and miss term paper deadlines
Supporting Facts and Examples:
—My friend Dan
—Cypress College study

Here is the finished paragraph.

1   Alcoholic beverages should be banned from college campuses, for two reasons. *The first reason is that drinking can cause academic failure.* If students drink* before class or have a hangover* from drinking too much the night before, they will be unable to concentrate* on their school work. They may miss classes, fail
5   exams, and miss term-paper deadlines. This behavior could force them to drop out of school. For example, last semester, my friend Dan, who liked to party every night, dropped out of school. He failed organic chemistry twice and barely passed his other classes. Therefore, his parents refused to pay for his education any longer. Recently, Cypress College did a study of student dropouts. Out of ninety cases
10   reported, 65 percent dropped out because they had failing grades due to excessive* drinking. Therefore, it is true that drinking can interfere* with college success.

Topic Sentence 2:
The second reason is that drinking and driving can be deadly.

The topic sentence in question form is, "Why is drinking and driving deadly?"

---

drink: here, drink alcohol
hangover: headache, sickness the day after drinking too much alcohol
concentrate: to keep all of one's thoughts, attention, or effort
excessive: too much   **interfere:** get in the way of

Try to think of main supporting ideas and supporting facts and examples for this reason.

Main Supporting Ideas:

_____

_____

_____

_____

_____

_____

Supporting Facts and Examples:

_____

_____

_____

_____

_____

_____

_____

_____

_____

_____

PRACTICE: Supporting Your Opinion

Choose one opinion (**a** or **b**) from each of the following pairs of thesis statements.

Brainstorm for reasons to support your thesis statement. Write down as many reasons as you can think of. Then, choose two of the best reasons from your brainstorming list to support your thesis statement. Write each of these reasons as a topic sentence.

Write down topic sentence 1. Brainstorm for specific details that will support it. You may ask yourself specific questions as the writer has done in the model paragraph above. The answers to these questions will help you to develop your paragraph to support the topic sentence. Follow this step for both paragraphs.

Remember to use sufficient specific details such as facts and examples to support each topic sentence.

1. a. It is a good idea for students to work part time while they are going to school.

   b. Students should not work while they are going to school.

2. a. Young people should continue to live with their parents after they finish their education.

   b. Young people should move away from home after they finish their education.

3. a. Physical education courses should be required in college.

   b. Physical education courses should not be required in college.

4. a. Women can successfully mix motherhood and careers.

   b. Women should not work if they have young children.

5. Students' own choice of an opinion topic.

Order of Importance

Refer to the model essay on page 155.

The first paragraph of the model essay is the introduction. It starts with several general statements and ends with the thesis statement:

> However, terminally ill patients should be allowed to die for several reasons.

The body of the essay discusses three reasons, and it discusses them in the order of their importance (in the opinion of the writer). The most important reason is discussed first, and the least important is discussed last. Writers often use this order. On the other hand, it is also effective to begin with the least important reason and build up to the most important at the end.

You can use either order in writing a persuasive essay. Just be sure you put your arguments in order of importance, either beginning or ending with the most important argument.

Transition Signals

We know which reason the writer of the model essay thinks is the most important one because of the transition phrase she has used in the topic sentence: "The first and most important reason . . . ." It is necessary to tell the reader in what order you are discussing your ideas, by using transition expressions that signal the order of things. The same transition expressions are used for time order and order of importance.

> The first reason is . . .
> The first and most important reason is . . .
> The second reason is . . .
> The final reason is . . .

Of course, if you discuss your most important reason last, your transition expression should be:

> The final and most important reason is . . .

The concluding paragraph of a persuasive essay is similar to any other conclusion:

- It ends the essay. (Use conclusion transition signals.)
- It summarizes the main reasons (or restates the thesis statement in different words).
- It may give the writer's final comment on the topic.

PRACTICE: Transition Signals

Review the model essay on page 155. Does the conclusion give a summary of the main reasons, or does it simply restate the thesis statement? What is the author's final comment? What conclusion transition expression does the author use? Circle all of the other transition signals you find in the essay. Which ones signal order of importance?

GRAMMAR

Modal Verbs

Modal verbs are words that add special meaning, like possibility, necessity, permission, and so on, to the main verbs that follow them. Modals include *can, could, will, would, shall, should, ought to, must, have to, may,* and *might.*

Modals have two forms: present and past, but the form of the modal does not necessarily express time in the sentence. Modals are *always* used with the simple form of the verb.

> Gerry might go to the hospital. (present or future)
> Andrew should take his medicine now. (present)
> You can/could see the doctor tomorrow. (future)

To make a sentence negative, add *not* to the modal. Most modals + *not* can be contracted.

Modal	Negative Form	Contraction
can	cannot	can't
could	could not	couldn't
shall	shall not	——
should	should not	shouldn't
must	must not	mustn't (Say: musn't)
may	may not	——
might	might not	——
will	will not	won't
would	would not	wouldn't

For example:

> I am sick. I shouldn't go out tonight.
> The doctor ordered me to stay home. I mustn't go out.

In questions, the modal form is written as follows:

> modal + subject + simple form of verb

> Will you drive to the beach?
> Should I take Highway 17?

In giving short answers to yes/no questions, the modal form is written as follows: *yes* or *no* + subject + modal.

> Will Gerry go with you?   Yes, he will.
>   No, he won't.
> Shouldn't your friend be here by now?   Yes, he should.
> Will you be here at six?   Yes, I will.

Now that you have learned the important forms of the modals, let us study their meanings and usage.

CAN

Can expresses ability and possibility.

> He can swim well. (ability)
> I can't solve the math problem. (inability)
> We can meet at the cafe at two. (possibility)

PRACTICE: *Can*

A. For each of the following items, write a statement in the first blank with the given information. Then in the second blank write a yes/no question from the statement.

1. (good swimmer/swim in the ocean)

    a. *A good swimmer can swim in the ocean.*

    b. *Can you swim in the ocean?*

2. (people/communicate with animals)

    a. _____

    b. _____

3. (robots/replace humans in auto factories)

    a. _____

    b. _____

4. (women/build houses)

    a. _____

    b. _____

5. (men/be good nurses)

    a. _____

    b. _____

6. (fathers/take good care of babies)

    a. _____

    b. _____

B. Write five original statements using the modal *can* to show ability. Write a question from each statement. Answer each question with *can* or *can't.*

COULD

Could expresses ability and possibility.

> We could leave now. (possibility)
> I couldn't go to school yesterday. (inability)
> I could speak Japanese when I was a child. (ability)

PRACTICE: *Could*

A. For each of the following items, write a statement in the first blank with the given information about what people could or couldn't do one hundred years ago. Then, in the second blank, write a yes/no question from the statement.

1. (people/fly to the moon)

    a. *People couldn't fly to the moon.*

    b. *Couldn't people fly to the moon? / Could people fly to the moon?*

2. (a person/get an artificial heart)

    a. _____

    b. _____

3. (a man/smoke in public)

    a. _____

    b. _____

4. (a woman/smoke in public)

    a. _____

    b. _____

5. (a woman/become president of her country)

    a. _____

    b. _____

6. (men/drink in bars)

    a. _____

    b. _____

B. Write five original sentences using the modal *could* to show ability.

MAY/MIGHT

May and *might* express possibility. They have the same meaning.

    She may go to Greece.
    She might be sick.

PRACTICE: *May/might*

Answer the following questions using the given information and a modal *may/might*.

1. Where are you going to school? (go to London)

I might go to London.

2. What is your sister going to do? (join the army)

3. Where are you going tonight? (go to a movie)

4. Are you taking anyone? (take my roommate)

5. When are you getting married? (get married in June)

6. Why didn't Gerry answer the phone? (be in the garage)

SHOULD/OUGHT TO

Should and *ought to* express the idea that the action in the main verb is good advice or a good idea.

You should stop smoking.
You ought to stop smoking.

PRACTICE: *Should/ought to*

A. Give advice using *should* or *ought to* in response to the following statements. When using the negative, use the contraction *shouldn't*. Use *you* as the subject of each sentence.

1. My car won't start.

You should check the gas.

2. I'm tired.

3. It looks like rain.

_____

4. I'm hungry.

_____

5. My neighbor's car is dirty.

_____

6. I haven't finished my homework for tomorrow, and I'm invited to a party tonight.

_____

7. I love Kathy. Kathy loves me.

_____

8. I need some money.

_____

9. I'm getting fat!

_____

B. Write five original sentences using _should/ought to_ and _shouldn't_, in which you tell someone to do or not to do something.

MUST/HAVE TO

Must and _have to_ express the idea of certainty or necessity (no choice).

> Students must come to class on time.
> I have to work tonight.

Must not or _mustn't_ (say: musn't) is the negative form of _must_.

> We mustn't be late for class.

Had to expresses necessity in the past. It is the past time form of both _must_ and _have to_.

> I had to work yesterday.

PRACTICE: *Should, must/have to, had to*

A. Fill in the blanks with the best modal and the verb in parentheses to complete the following sentences.

> Reminder:
> *should/ought to*: the idea is a good one; the action will probably happen (almost certain)
> *must/have to*: the action is certain or necessary (present/future time)
> *had to*: the action was necessary (past time)

1. Where is your homework?

It (be) _must be_____ at home.

2. I have a bad cold.

You (stay) _____ at home.

3. Why didn't you come to class yesterday?

I (go) _____ on an art class field trip.

4. I can't go to the party tonight.

I (study) _____.

5. I didn't understand today's lecture.

You (talk) _____ to the teacher.

6. John is getting married soon.

He (give up) _____ all of his girl-friends.

7. I'm not doing well in my English class.

You (study) _____ harder.

B. Fill in the blanks with the best modals and main verbs to complete the following sentences. Watch out for the verb tenses of the given sentences.

1. I wonder why Susan doesn't answer the phone.

She _must be_____ in the shower.

2. Do you have the time?

No, I don't, but it _____ about 10:15.

3. I didn't see you at the party last night. What happened?

Oh, I _____.

4. I didn't go skiing last weekend.
Why not?

I had two tests on Monday, so I _____.

5. I feel awful. I can't sleep or eat.

You _____ the doctor right away!

6. George works sixty hours a week. He looks tired.

He _____ more often.

7. I didn't pass my computer science test last week.
Why not?

I didn't have time to study. I probably _____ my job.

C. Write six original sentences with modals as follows: two with *should/ought to*, two with *must/have to*, and two with *had to*.

WILL

Will expresses future action. It means the same as *be going to* + simple verb. Contractions with subject pronouns and nouns + *will* are formed like *I'll, he'll, John'll*, and so on.

She will leave for Europe next week.
Robots will do many boring tasks at home and in industry.

PRACTICE: Using Modals

A. Fill in the blanks with the best modals to complete the following paragraphs. Choose from *must, will, can, has to, may/might,* and *should.* Also, use negative modal forms and contractions where it is possible.

Going Camping

1   American people of all ages love to go camping. They sleep and eat outdoors at beaches and in the mountains. They love to enjoy nature at its best.

My classmates and I are going camping next weekend. This _____

5 be my first camping trip, and I am looking forward to it. My roommates Juan

and Peter are not sure they _____ go. Their parents

_____ visit them. Maybe they _____ ask

their parents to visit the following weekend. I _____ be

disappointed if they _____ go.

10   We _____ take lots of food and equipment for our trip.

For example, because we _____ sleep outdoors, we

_____ take our sleeping bags and a tent. We also

_____ remember to take extra blankets because the nights

are cold. We _____ cook all of our meals on an outdoor

15 barbecue. Therefore, we _____ forget to bring wood, char-

coal, and, of course, matches.

     We _____ go fishing and swimming in the lake, so we

_____ remember to bring our bathing suits. Otherwise, we

_____ go swimming.

20   In brief, we _____ have a great time, and we are all

looking forward to this camping trip. Juan and Peter _____

be sorry if they don't go with us.

B. Add a modal + a main verb to the following sentences. The meaning of the modal you should use is given in parentheses after each sentence.

1. It's cold today.

   You *should wear* _____ your overcoat. (good idea)

2. Can you pick me up at the downtown station?

   No, I'm sorry I _____. (impossibility)

   _____ you _____ a taxi? (possibility)

3. I'm gaining weight!

   You _____ so much. (not a good idea)

4. I had a bad cold last week. I still don't feel well.

   You _____ at home. (good idea)

5. The plane leaves in a couple of hours.

   We _____ for the airport now! (necessity)

6. I don't have any money.

   Ask Dad. He _____ you some. (possibility)

7. Can Alan type fast?

   No, he _____ only

   _____ forty words a minute. (ability)

8. Why didn't you come to class this morning?

   I overslept. I _____ until 2:00 A.M. (necessity)

9. Will you go to the tennis match with us?

   Yes, I _____. (future action)

10. It's a beautiful day. Where do you want to go?

We _____ to the park. (possibility)

11. My television set is broken.

I _____ it for you. (ability)

FREEWRITING

Write a letter to a friend in another country and tell him or her why he or she should visit your city or country. In your letter, tell your friend the names of some interesting places to visit, wonderful restaurants to enjoy, and day and evening activities to take part in. Use modals where they are appropriate.

SENTENCE STRUCTURE

Three kinds of clauses are useful when you write a persuasive essay: reason, contrast, and result clauses. The following chart lists the transition signals that introduce these kinds of clauses. The transition signals are classified into three groups: sentence connectors, coordinators, and subordinators.

Kind of Clause	Transition Signals		
	Sentence Connectors	Coordinators	Subordinators
Reason (to give reasons)			because since as
Contrast (to add opposite ideas)	however nevertheless	but	even though although
Result (to give results or effects)	therefore consequently	so	

Reason Clauses

Reason clauses answer the question Why?

Because, since, and *as* are subordinators that introduce dependent reason clauses. They give the reason for the idea in the independent clause. The reason clause can come before or after the independent clause.

Example:

Volcanoes are always dangerous. (statement)
Why are volcanoes always dangerous?
... because they give no warning signals. (reason)
Volcanoes are always dangerous because they give no warning signals.
Because volcanoes give no warning signals, they are always dangerous.

Remember the comma rule: If the dependent clause comes at the beginning of a sentence, use a comma.

PRACTICE: Reason Clauses

A. Read each of the following pairs of sentences carefully. Choose the clause that gives the reason for the other clause. Then add a subordinator to the reason clause and write a new sentence by combining the reason clause with the independent clause. Use correct punctuation.

NOTE: When the subjects (or objects) of both clauses are the same, use a noun in the first clause and a pronoun in the second clause.

1. Pollution is a problem.
   Pollution affects our health. (reason)

   Pollution is a problem because it affects our health.

   or

   Because pollution affects our health, it is a problem.

2. Noise is a form of pollution.
   Noise can damage our health.

   _____

   _____

3. Noise is harmful to the body.
   Noise can change the heart rate* and increase blood pressure*.

   _____

   _____

4. The mother's body reacts to noise.
   Noise can affect an unborn baby.

   _____

   _____

---

heart rate: how fast a heart beats   **blood pressure:** the force of blood through the body

5. The noise level near a school should not be high.
Children need a quiet environment to learn in.

_____

_____

6. Noise is a serious problem.
No one can escape from noise.

_____

_____

B. Complete the following sentences with a reason clause or an independent clause. Use correct punctuation.

1. Riding a bicycle is popular because ___*it is good exercise.*___

2. Bicycles are more economical than cars since _____

_____

3. Bicycling is good exercise because _____

_____

4. Since _____
parking is not a problem.

5. Riding a bicycle is better than driving because _____

_____

6. Because I can't afford to buy a car _____

_____

C. Write four original sentences using the reason subordinators *because* twice and *since* twice.

Contrast Clauses

Contrast clauses are independent or dependent clauses that present an idea that contrasts with another idea in the sentence.

However and *nevertheless* are sentence connectors that introduce contrast clauses. They connect the idea in the first clause with a contrasting idea in the second clause. These sentence connectors tell the reader that an opposite idea from the first clause will follow. *However* and *nevertheless* have the same meaning as the coordinator *but*. Both *however* and *nevertheless* should be followed by a comma. (Review the punctuation of sentence connectors on page 84.)

Example:
A motorcycle is fun to ride. (statement)
A motorcycle can be dangerous. (contrasting or opposite idea)
A motorcycle is fun to ride; however, it can be dangerous.

PRACTICE: Contrast Clauses

A. Read each of the following pairs of sentences carefully. Write the most logical clause as the first clause. Then, add a sentence connector and write the second clause. Use correct punctuation.

1. A secondhand* one is reasonable.
The cost of a new motorcycle is high.

_____

_____

2. Young people don't worry about that.
A motorcycle doesn't protect the rider.

_____

_____

3. Motorcyclists should wear helmets*.
Many of them don't like to wear helmets.

_____

_____

4. My parents won't let me buy one.
I want to buy a motorcycle.

_____

_____

5. I also want a motorcycle.
I own a sports car.

_____

_____

B. Write four original sentences using the sentence connectors *however* twice and *nevertheless* twice.

---

secondhand: not new
helmet: hard hat to protect the head

Although and even though are subordinators that introduce a dependent clause showing a contrast to the idea in the independent clause. They have the same meaning as the sentence connectors however and nevertheless.

The although or even though clause can come at the beginning of the sentence or after the independent clause.

Example:

Although I should buy a car, I want to buy a motorcycle.
I want to buy a motorcycle although I should buy a car.

PRACTICE: Contrast Clauses

A. Rewrite the sentences in Practice A on page 173 using the subordinators although and even though. You may place the contrast clause either before or after the independent clause.

1. *Although the cost of a new motorcycle is high,* a secondhand one is reasonable.

 or

 A secondhand motorcycle is reasonable *even though the cost of a new one is high.*

2. _____

 _____

3. _____

 _____

4. _____

 _____

B. Write four original sentences using although twice and even though twice.

Result Clauses

Result clauses are independent clauses that tell the result of something described in the first independent clause.

Therefore and *consequently* are sentence connectors that connect two independent clauses when the second clause is the result of the first clause. They have the same meaning as the coordinator *so*. Both *therefore* and *consequently* should be followed by a comma.

Example:
Marriage is back in style. (statement)
Many couples are taking the big step*. (result)
Marriage is back in style; therefore, many couples are taking the big step.

PRACTICE: Result Clauses

A. Read each of the following pairs of sentences carefully. Choose the clause that gives the result. Then combine the sentences, and add *therefore* or *consequently* before the result clause. Punctuate the sentences correctly.

1. Marriage is not easy.
A couple should work hard to make it successful.

_____

_____

2. Their husbands should help with the housework.
Many women continue to work after marriage.

_____

_____

3. Many married women earn high salaries.
Their husbands don't have to worry about paying all the bills.

_____

_____

4. Some married women take care of all the housework and cooking.
Some married women don't work outside the home.

_____

_____

---

taking the big step: making a big decision (idiom)

5. Many young couples have unrealistic* ideas about marriage. Many marriages end in divorce.

_____

_____

B. Complete the following sentences using the sentence connectors *consequently* or *therefore*. Choose the best clause to complete each sentence from the following list. Use correct punctuation.

I can speak with Americans better   I have a lot more confidence
We had a lot of practice   The teacher tried to help us
My friends didn't understand me before   We all had to speak English
We were nervous   We weren't nervous

1. Last semester I took an English conversation class; _therefore, I_

can speak with Americans better.

2. We had to speak English all the time _____

_____

3. The teacher told us not to worry about our mistakes _____

_____

4. My classmates were from many countries of the world _____

_____

5. We couldn't pronounce the "th" sounds like in "thank" and "think"

_____

6. I learned a lot in my conversation class _____

_____

PRACTICE: Sentence Completion

Complete the following sentences with your own ideas. Use correct punctuation.

1. I want to travel around the world; however, _I don't have the_

time or money.

2. I don't have the money therefore _____

_____

unrealistic: impractical, unreasonable

3. My friends are going to Paris and London nevertheless _____

_____

4. I would like to go because _____

_____

5. Even though traveling is expensive _____

_____

6. I asked my parents for the money but _____

_____

7. My parents refused to give me the money so _____

_____

8. Since traveling is educational _____

_____

ON YOUR OWN!

Write a persuasive essay. First, choose a topic sentence from the following list. Choose only *one* position from the two presented. Before you write, brainstorm your topic and develop an outline. Your instructor may want to check your outline.

1. A married father should/should not be responsible for taking care of his child (or children).
2. Ordinary citizens should/should not be allowed to carry handguns*.
3. Television networks* should/should not present children's cartoons that show violence.
4. High school education should be/should not be free.
5. Women should/should not serve in the military service.
6. A couple should/should not live together before marriage.

Hints for Success

■ Do the prewriting activities:
  1. Brainstorm for reasons and supporting details.
  2. Make an outline.
■ Write your first draft, and check it against the essay checklist on page 102.
  1. Check your organization.
  2. Check your sentence structure.

handguns: small guns that one can hold in the hand
television networks: television companies

chapter 10

Comparison and Contrast

Model: The Changing American Family

1   The family is important to people all over the world although the structure of
the family is quite different from one country to another. In the United States, as
in many countries in the world, the family is changing. A generation* or two
ago, the traditional family, in which the father was boss, was customary. Now, the
5   modern family, in which both the father and the mother are equal partners, is more
common. Although there are several similarities between the traditional and the
modern family, there are also some very important differences.

   The traditional family of yesterday and the modern family of today have
several similarities. The traditional family was a nuclear family,* and the modern
10   family is, too. The role* of the father in the traditional family was to provide for his
family. Similarly, the father in the modern family is expected to do so, also. The
mother in the traditional family took care of the children's physical and emotional
needs just as the modern mother does.

   On the other hand, there are some great differences between the traditional
15   family and the modern family. The first important difference is in the man's role. The
traditional husband was the head of the household because he was the only one
who worked outside the home. If the wife worked for pay, then the husband was not
considered to be a good provider. In many families today, both husband and wife
work for pay. Therefore, they share the role of head of household. In addition, the
20   traditional husband usually made the big decisions about spending money.
However, the modern husband shares these decisions with his working wife. Also,
the traditional husband did not help his wife with the housework or meal
preparation. Dinner was ready when he came home. In contrast, the modern

---

generation: period of time between parents and children, usually considered to be about
  thirty-three years
nuclear family: father, mother, and children
role: part one plays (in a drama, in a family, etc.)

husband helps his working wife at home. He may do some of the household jobs,
25 and it is not unusual for him to cook.

The second difference is in the woman's role. In the traditional family, the
woman may have worked for pay during her first years of marriage. However, after
she became pregnant*, she would usually quit her job. Her primary role was to take
care of her family and home. In contrast, in many families today, the modern
30 woman works outside the home even after she has children. She is doing two jobs
instead of one, so she is busier than the traditional mother was. The traditional wife
learned to live within her husband's income. On the other hand, the modern wife
does not have to because the family has two incomes.

The final difference is in the role of the children. In the traditional family, the
35 children were taken care of by the mother because she did not work outside the
home. However, today preschool* children may go to a child care center or to a
babysitter* regularly because the mother works. The school-age children of a
traditional family were more dependent. Their mother was there to help them to get
ready for school and to make their breakfast. In contrast, modern children are more
40 independent. They have to get up early in the morning and get ready for school.
Their mother is busy getting ready for work, so they may even have to make their
own breakfast.

In conclusion, the American family of today is different from the family of fifty
years ago. In the modern family, the roles of the father, mother, and children have
45 changed as more and more women work outside the home. The next century* may
bring more important changes to the American family structure. It should be
interesting to see.

Questions on the Model

1. What are the two kinds of families in the United States?
2. How are the roles of the men in both families different?
3. How are the roles of the women different?
4. How are the children's roles different?
5. What is the thesis statement in the model composition?
6. Which paragraph explains the similarities between the traditional and nuclear families? How many similarities are discussed?
7. How many paragraphs explain the differences?
8. What is the purpose of the last paragraph?

ORGANIZATION

Overview of Comparison and Contrast

In this chapter you will learn how to organize a comparison and contrast composition.

When you compare two things, you point out their similarities. When you contrast two things, you point out their differences. For example, you can compare two cars, two teachers, two jobs, two ways to

---

pregnant: about to have a baby
babysitter: person who is paid to take care of children
preschool: before age five
century: one hundred years

spend a weekend, and so on. Here are some important points to remember when writing about the similarities and differences between two items.

- The items that you compare and/or contrast must be from the same general class. So, you could compare a sports car with a station wagon, but you wouldn't compare a car with a sailboat.
- When you write about the two items, be sure the features or points you use for support apply to both things. For instance, if you write about the atmosphere, service, and menu at restaurant A, you must also discuss these points about restaurant B.
- The thesis sentence should clearly state both the subjects and the controlling idea. It can also name the subpoints for the comparison and/or contrast.

Notice the following examples of thesis statements comparing two cars:

The Super XL and the Magna XL are alike in several ways. (comparison)

The Super XL and the Magna XL have some very important differences. (contrast)

The Super XL and the Magna XL have both similarities and differences. (comparison/contrast)

The Super XL and the Magna XL are different in the following areas: exterior design, interior design, and comfort. (contrast)

Study the model essay on pages 179–180 and notice how the essay is organized:

I. Introduction
(paragraph 1)

> General statements
> Thesis statement

II. Body
(paragraph 2)

> Similarities

(paragraph 3)

> The first difference
> (man's role)

(paragraph 4)

> The second difference
> (woman's role)

(paragraph 5)

> The third difference
> (children's role)

III. Conclusion
(paragraph 6)

> Main points
> Final comments

The writer begins the essay with general background statements to present the topic of the essay, the changing American family. The first paragraph ends with the thesis statement, which tells the reader that first similarities and then differences will be discussed:

> Although there are several similarities between the traditional and the modern family, there are also some very important differences.

The first sentence of each body paragraph is a topic sentence, which states the topic and the controlling idea for each of these paragraphs. It is followed by specific details that support its controlling idea.

The topic sentence for paragraph 2 states that similarities between the traditional and the modern family will be discussed.

> The traditional family of yesterday and the modern family of today have several similarities.

The next three paragraphs (3, 4, and 5) discuss the differences between the traditional and the modern family. The transition expression that begins paragraph 3, *on the other hand*, shifts the discussion of the essay from the similarities to the differences between the two kinds of families. It is followed by the first topic sentence regarding differences.

> On the other hand, there are some great differences between the traditional family and the modern family. The first important difference is in the man's role.

Each of paragraphs 4 and 5 also begins with a transition expression that introduces a specific difference.

> The second difference is in the woman's role.
> The final difference is in the role of the children.

The last paragraph is a conclusion, which ends the essay with a summary of the main points. Then, the writer adds a final comment.

> Summary of main points:
> In conclusion, the American family of today is different from the family of fifty years ago. In the modern family, the roles of the father, mother, and children have changed as more and more women work outside the home.
> Final comment:
> The next century may bring more important changes to the American family structure. It should be interesting to see.

Block Organization

A comparison and contrast composition can be organized in several ways. However, in this book, you will learn the most basic pattern of comparison and contrast organization. It is called **block organization.**

In block organization, the similarities are discussed together in one block (which can be one paragraph or several paragraphs). Then, the differences are discussed together in one block. So, block organization looks like this:

```
┌─────────────────────────────────┐
│ Similarities                    │
│                                 │
│     Point 1 for A and B         │
│     Point 2 for A and B         │
│     Point 3 for A and B         │
│     Point 4 for A and B         │
└─────────────────────────────────┘

┌─────────────────────────────────┐
│ Differences                     │
│                                 │
│     Point 1 for A and B         │
│     Point 2 for A and B         │
│     Point 3 for A and B         │
│     Point 4 for A and B         │
└─────────────────────────────────┘
```

Example:

Alaska and Hawaii have several similarities.

I. Similarities

    A. The environments* of both Alaska and Hawaii are the same.

        1. Unpolluted skies in Alaska and Hawaii

        2. Natural landscapes* in Alaska and Hawaii

        3. Unpolluted waters in Alaska and Hawaii

    B. There are great natural wonders* in both states.

        1. Chugach Mountains and Mt. McKinley in Alaska

        2. Volcano National Park and Waimea Canyon in Hawaii

On the other hand, there are several important differences between vacationing in Alaska and Hawaii.

II. Differences

    A. The climate in Alaska is different from the climate in Hawaii.

        1. The temperatures in Alaska and Hawaii

        2. The rainfall in Alaska and Hawaii

        3. The humidity* in Alaska and Hawaii

    B. The tours to these famous states are also different.

        1. Cruise ship* to Alaska and jumbo* jet to Hawaii

        2. Transportation within Alaska and Hawaii

    C. Alaska's and Hawaii's accommodations are not the same.

        1. Hotels in Alaska and Hawaii

        2. Meals in Alaska and Hawaii

You can, of course, discuss the differences first and then the similarities.

---

environment: surroundings, everything that is around you
landscape: scenery
natural wonders: places of great geologic interest on earth
humidity: amount of water in the air
cruise ship: vacation ship   **jumbo:** very large

GRAMMAR AND MECHANICS

Adjectives and Adverbs of Comparison

When you are comparing two or more things, adjectives and adverbs of comparison are useful. You use the **comparative** form of an adjective or adverb to show the differences between two things. You use the **superlative** form of an adjective or adverb to show how one thing differs from two or more things.

ONE-SYLLABLE ADJECTIVES AND ADVERBS

Most adjectives and adverbs of only one syllable form their comparative and superlative forms as follows:

- Comparative: Add *-er than* to compare two things.
- Superlative: Add *the -est* to compare three or more things.

	Adjective	Adverb
Base word form:	old	fast
Comparative:	older than	faster than
Superlative:	the oldest	the fastest

Examples:

John is twenty years old. Bill is eighteen years old. Tom is twenty-two years old.
John is older than Bill. Tom is the oldest in the family.

Tom ran two miles in fifteen minutes. Bill ran two miles in sixteen minutes. John ran two miles in twelve minutes.
Tom ran faster than Bill. John ran the fastest in the race.

PRACTICE: Comparative and Superlative Forms

Fill in the following blanks with (a) the comparative and (b) the superlative forms of the underlined words.

1. Yesterday was <u>hot</u> in Chicago.

   a. It was _____ the day before.

   b. It was _____ day so far this summer.

2. The history test was <u>hard</u>.

   a. It was _____ the last test.

   b. It was _____ test this semester.

3. The climate here is <u>warm</u>.

    a. It is _____ the climate in Mexico City.

    b. In fact, it is _____ climate in the world.

4. My mother is a very <u>wise</u> woman.

    a. Of course, she is _____ my father.

    b. But the truth is, my grandfather is _____ person in the family.

5. Ching is learning English <u>fast</u>.

    a. He is learning it _____ his brother.

    b. But he isn't _____ learner in his class.

ADJECTIVES AND ADVERBS OF TWO OR MORE SYLLABLES

Most adjectives and adverbs of two or more syllables form their comparative and superlative forms as follows:

- Comparative: *more/less* + adjective/adverb *than*
- Superlative: *the most/least* + adjective/adverb

	Adjective	Adverb
Base word form:	interesting	carefully
Comparative:	more/less interesting than	more/less carefully than
Superlative:	the most/least interesting	the most/least carefully

Example:

The president is a famous person.
He is more famous than the vice president.
He is the most famous person in the United States.

EXCEPTIONS: Two-syllable words ending in *-y*, *-le*, *-er*, and *-ow*, and the adjective *friendly* (*friendlier, friendliest*) form their comparative and superlative forms more like one-syllable adjectives and adverbs.

	-y	-le	-er	-ow
Base word form:	easy	gentle	clever	narrow
Comparative:	easier	gentler	cleverer	narrower
Superlative:	easiest	gentlest	cleverest	narrowest

Example:
A working woman is busy.
A married woman is busier than a working woman.
But a working mother is the busiest of all.

NOTE: *of all* is usually added after a superlative adverb or adjective if the noun is omitted.

PRACTICE: Comparative and Superlative Forms

Complete the following sentences with verbs and the comparative and superlative forms of the underlined words.

1. My dad bought me a new car. He is a very <u>generous</u> man.

   a. He _____ John's father.

   b. I think he _____ person in the world.

2. Soul music* is <u>popular</u> among young people.

   a. Jazz music _____ soul music among young people.

   b. Rock and roll music _____ among young people. (Add *of all.*)

3. Tokyo was <u>smoggy</u> last weekend.

   a. Mexico City _____ Tokyo.

   b. New York City _____ of all.

4. I think American food is <u>tasty</u>.

   a. Vong thinks Chinese food _____ American food.

   b. But Gino thinks Italian food _____ .

5. Watching soccer on TV is <u>exciting</u>.

   a. Watching a live soccer game _____ .

   b. Playing soccer _____ .

---

soul music: a kind of music developed by American black musicians in the 1960s

6. Houses in Dallas are <u>expensive</u>.

    a. Houses (less) _____ in Miami.

    b. Houses (least) _____ in Phoenix.

7. Traffic moves <u>slowly</u> in the city on Friday afternoons.

    a. It _____ on the freeways*.

    b. It _____ across the bridge.

8. Yoshiko has learned English conversation <u>rapidly</u>.

    a. She _____ her sister.

    b. However, Conchita _____

    _____ in their class.

9. Stockholm's winters are <u>chilly</u>.

    a. They _____ Helsinki's winters.

    b. But Moscow's winters _____.

10. Big diesel trucks are <u>noisy</u>.

    a. Diesel trucks (less) _____ trains.

    b. Jet planes _____ of all.

IRREGULAR ADJECTIVES AND ADVERBS

Four words have irregular comparative and superlative forms: *good, bad, little,* and *well.*

Base word form:	good	bad	little	well
Comparative:	better than	worse than	less than	better than
Superlative:	the best	the worst	the least	the best

Example:
Blanca is a good tennis player.
She is better than most of the team players.
However, she isn't the best player on the team.

---

freeway: road without stop signs or stop lights

PRACTICE: Irregular Forms

Fill in the blanks in the following sentences with the correct irregular forms of the underlined words.

1. Jean is a <u>good</u> singer.

    a. She sings _____ Pat.

    b. The director thinks she is _____ singer in the musical show.

2. Mary had only a <u>little</u> wine at the party.

    a. She drank _____ I did.

    b. She drank only a half a glass, so she drank _____ of all of us.

3. My history essay received a <u>bad</u> grade.

    a. It was _____ Carl's grade.

    b. But it certainly wasn't _____ grade in the class.

4. Ron ran <u>well</u> in the marathon.

    a. He ran _____ Jimmy.

    b. But Ron didn't run _____ in his group.

5. Smoking is a <u>bad</u> habit.

    a. Drinking too much is _____.

    b. Drinking and driving is _____ of all.

6. After our team lost the World's Cup, everybody in the nation felt <u>bad</u>.

    a. The soccer coach felt _____ the fans did.

    b. But the soccer players felt _____ of all.

7. I like to ski <u>frequently</u>.

    a. I ski _____ than Kanako and Reiko.

    b. However, Kimiko skis _____ of all.

PRACTICE: Comparison Chart

Fill in the blanks to complete the chart that follows.

Base Word	Comparative	Superlative
1. young	younger than	the youngest
2. _____	_____	the most popular
3. _____	sleepier than	_____
4. important	_____	_____
5. _____	cooler than	_____
6. _____	_____	the smallest
7. busy	_____	_____
8. _____	prettier than	_____
9. _____	better than	_____
10. well	_____	_____
11. _____	_____	the worst
12. _____	more famous than	_____
13. _____	_____	the laziest
14. clever	_____	_____
15. carefully	_____	_____
16. _____	_____	the richest
17. interesting	_____	_____
18. _____	thinner than	_____
19. healthy	_____	_____
20. exciting	_____	_____
21. happy	_____	_____
22. _____	more studious than	_____
23. _____	_____	the sunniest

COMPARISONS USING *AS . . . AS*

When the two items you are comparing are similar on a certain point, you can use *as* + adjective/adverb + *as* to show it.

Examples:

I pay seven hundred dollars a month for my apartment.
Jose pays seven hundred dollars a month for his apartment.
My apartment is as expensive as Jose's apartment.
My apartment is as cheap as Jose's apartment.
Tony drove to the beach in two hours.
Ryan made it in two hours, too.
Ryan drove to the beach as fast as Tony did.

To show that two things are not equal, you can use *not as* adjective/adverb + *as*.

Examples:

My Mercedes 450SL cost $40,000.
My brother's Maseratti cost $55,000. (expensive)
My car isn't as expensive as my brother's car.
My mother-in-law cooks well.
My husband burns everything.
My husband doesn't cook as well as my mother-in-law.

PRACTICE: *As . . . as*

Fill in the blanks in the following sentences with a form of *as . . . as* or *not as . . . as*. Use the given word or the underlined word.

1. My boss works from nine to five. I do too.

The boss works (hard) _____.

2. Kathleen eats out four times a week. Gerry eats out every day.

Kathleen (often) _____.

3. Bianca is thirty-nine years old. Her husband is forty-two years old.

Bianca (old) _____.

4. The peaches are <u>sweet and juicy</u>. The plums are hard and sour.

The plums (ripe) _____.

5. Salvador finished the test. David finished it at the same time.

Salvador finished the test (fast) _____
David did.

6. My grandfather eats <u>slowly</u>. My son does, too.

My grandfather eats _____ my son does.

7. Young male drivers get a lot of speeding tickets. Young female drivers don't.

Young male drivers (carefully) _____

_____ .

Young female drivers (recklessly) _____

_____ .

PRACTICE: Comparative and Superlative Forms

A. The following sentences have comparative and superlative form errors. Cross out each error and write the correct form above it.

1. Football is the ~~mostest~~ *most* exciting spectator sport.

2. Chiang is more taller than I am.

3. The female comedian was the most funniest performer in the show.

4. My uncle is more rich than my father.

5. Our new neighbors are noisiest than our old neighbors.

6. Janet wore the most pretty dress at the party.

7. These cookies are the bestest I have ever eaten.

8. The final history test was the worser one we had all semester.

9. Los Angeles is more far west than San Francisco.

10. Tokyo has the larger population in the world.

11. Skiing last winter was a lot gooder than it was this year.

12. The vegetables at Super Market are more fresh and more expensiver than at Grand Market.

13. Alicia's English grade was gooder than mine. In fact, it was the bestest grade in the class.

B. Add the comparative or superlative form of the given word to complete the following sentences.

1. Tony is a good football player. He is playing (well) _____

   this season than last season. In fact, this is his (good) _____

   season of all.

2. London has cool weather in the summer. Most of the time, it is

   (fog) _____ in the evenings than in the mornings.

   Sometimes it is so cold that tourists have remarked, "This is the

   (bad) _____ city in the world to visit in June."

3. I have two dogs. Koki weighs ninety pounds, while Toby weighs forty

   pounds. Koki is two years (young) _____ Toby and

   weighs fifty pounds more. It is (easy) _____ for me to

   walk Toby than Koki because Toby has (short) _____

   legs. Toby is (obedient) _____ than Koki, and Koki is

   (lively) _____ than Toby. On the other hand, Koki is

   (handsome) _____ and a (good) _____

   watchdog than Toby. They are very different from each other. I love

   them both, but I can only walk one dog at a time.

Comparative and Superlative Forms with Nouns

Comparative and superlative forms are used not only with adjectives and adverbs but also with nouns. *More/the most, fewer/the fewest,* and *less/the least* are used with nouns to compare amount, number, or degree.

More and *the most* are used with nouns as follows:

■ Comparative: *more* + (noun) + *than* (a greater number or amount)
■ Superlative: *the most* + noun (*of all*) (the greatest number or amount)

> There are more people in Tokyo than (there are) in New York City.
> Shanghai has the most people in the world.

Fewer and *fewest* are used with nouns as follows:

■ Comparative: *fewer* + (noun) + *than* (a smaller number of something that can be counted)
■ Superlative: *the fewest* + noun (*of all*) (the smallest number of something that can be counted)

> There are fewer cars per family in Japan than (there are) in the United States.
> China has the fewest cars, but it has the most bicycles.

Less and *least* are used with nouns as follows:

■ Comparative: *less* + (noun) + *than* (a smaller amount of something that cannot be counted)
■ Superlative: *the least* + noun (*of all*) (the smallest amount of something that cannot be counted)

> Nowadays, some men make less money than women in the same job.
> Teenagers make the least money.

PRACTICE: Comparative and Superlative Forms

Fill in the blanks in the following sentences with the correct comparative or superlative form.

CAUTION: Use the correct forms for things that can be counted and things that cannot be counted.

1. My new apartment has (greater amount) _____*more*_____ sunlight than my old one. However, it has (smaller number) _____ rooms. Now, I pay $550 per month. I paid $585 for my last apartment. So, I pay (smaller amount) _____ rent now. Therefore, I can save (greater amount) _____ money to buy a new sofa for my living room. The one I want costs (greater amount) _____ $700. Right now, I have (smaller amount) _____ $200 in the bank. However, I should be able to buy the new sofa in (smaller number) _____ six months.

2. Fat people usually eat (greater amount) _____ food than thin people. They don't realize that the (smaller amount) _____ they eat the (smaller amount) _____ weight they will gain. Cakes, candy, and cookies have (greatest number) _____ calories. Moreover, dieters should avoid sugar and honey. In fact, honey is as bad as sugar. Vegetables have (smallest number) _____ calories of all. Fruits and vegetables are (smallest amount) _____ expensive of all foods. Many overweight people eat lots of junk food. They are probably (smaller amount) _____ interested in nutritious food _____ people who watch their diets.

DICTOCOMP

Write this paragraph as your teacher dictates it to you.

Taking a Vacation

1   This summer Antonio, who is from Brazil, and his classmate Pierre, who is from France, want to spend two weeks in either Alaska or Hawaii. Antonio wants to go to Alaska, but Pierre prefers Hawaii. Antonio thinks that Alaska is more interesting than Hawaii because there are ice-capped mountains, glaciers*, and wild animals.
5 Pierre, on the other hand, wants to go to Hawaii because the climate is milder and the lifestyle is more relaxed. He is less interested in watching wild animals than in watching wild hula dancers! Also, a trip to Hawaii is less expensive than a trip to Alaska, so the two classmates have decided that Hawaii is the best place to go.

glacier: river of ice

FREEWRITING

Write as many sentences as you can comparing and contrasting the items in each set of pictures above.

SENTENCE STRUCTURE

Comparison Structure Words and Phrases

When you want to compare something within a sentence or between two sentences, comparison structure words and phrases are useful. These words and phrases connect the two parts of a comparison of two items, places, persons, and so on. The following table gives a partial list of the most common words and phrases that are used to show similarities.

COMPARISON STRUCTURE WORDS AND PHRASES

Sentence Connectors	Conjunctions		Others	Paired Conjunctions
	Coordinating	**Subordinating**		
similarly	and . . . (too)	just as	just like	both . . . and
likewise			the same	not only . . . but also
			alike	
also			similar to	
too			the same as	

Let's study each group of comparison structure words and phrases.

■ Sentence connectors are used to show the connection between two complete sentences or independent clauses:

$$\text{Independent clause.} \quad \begin{matrix} Also, \\ Similarly, \\ Likewise, \end{matrix} + \text{independent clause.}$$

Notice the comma after the sentence connector.

Tokyo is an exciting city. Similarly, New York City is an exciting city.

Tokyo is an exciting city. Likewise, New York City is an exciting city.

The word *too* is usually placed at the end of the second sentence or independent clause:

Independent clause. Independent clause, *too.*

Notice the comma before *too.*

Tokyo is an exciting city. New York City is an exciting city, too.

■ Subordinating conjunctions are used to show a comparison between two clauses, one independent and one dependent:

New York City is a crowded, noisy city just as Tokyo is.

■ Coordinating conjunctions are used to show a comparison between two independent clauses:

Independent clause, + *and* + independent clause, + *too.*

Tokyo has many skyscrapers, and New York City does, too.

■ Other comparison structure words and phrases are used to show comparisons within sentences.

Tokyo is just like New York City in many respects. (preposition)

Tokyo's traffic is similar to New York City's traffic. (preposition) There are many taxis, buses, and cars, which cause huge traffic jams.

The streets in downtown Tokyo and New York City are <u>alike</u>. (adjective)

> They are wide and dangerous.

The subway system in New York City is <u>the same as</u> the one in Tokyo. (noun + preposition)

> Both systems carry thousands of people daily to distant points of these huge metropolitan areas*.

The shopping areas are <u>the same</u>. (noun phrase)

> There are big, top quality department stores, numerous boutiques, and even street merchants.

■ Paired conjunctions are always used together. Notice that the word that comes after the second conjunction must be the same part of speech (noun, verb, prepositional phrase, etc.) as the word that comes after the first conjunction. This is an important rule in English and is called the rule of **parallelism.**

RIGHT: The two cities are both noisy [adjective] and crowded [adjective].

WRONG: The two cities are both busy [adjective] and have too many people [verb phrase].

Both New York City and Tokyo have outstanding international restaurants. (nouns)

Tokyoites and New Yorkers can both eat and drink almost anything. (verbs)

The two cities have both positive and negative features. (adjectives)

Not only Tokyoites but also New Yorkers dress fashionably. (nouns)

You can see joggers not only in Central Park but also in Hibuya Park. (prepositional phrases)

PRACTICE: Paired Conjunctions

Complete the following sentences. Be sure to follow the rule of parallelism.

1. Both in Tokyo and *in New York City* _____ the art museums display many famous masterpieces.

2. Both overcrowded subways and _____ are problems in Tokyo and New York City.

3. You can buy designer clothes not only in boutiques but also

_____ .

---

metropolitan area: large city and surrounding towns

4. New Yorkers and Tokyoites not only can see a movie at any time but also _____.

5. In the summer, the weather in Tokyo and in New York is both hot and _____.

6. The Ginza and Fifth Avenue shopping districts have both fine jewelers and _____.

PRACTICE: Using Comparison Structure Words and Phrases

Write a new sentence comparing the two sentences in each of the following pairs, using the given comparison structure words. Punctuate correctly.

1. Advertising brings the public information about a product or a service. It is used to sell an idea or an event. (similarly)

Advertising brings the public information about a product;

similarly, it is used to sell an idea or an event.

2. Advertisements influence* a person's choice of food and other daily necessities. They influence a person's choice of a vacation spot and restaurant. (not only . . . but also)

_____

_____

3. Advertising influences people's spending habits. It raises their standard of living. (both . . . and)

_____

_____

4. To buy new products, people will work harder. They will spend their money wisely. (also)

_____

_____

influence: to have an effect on

5. Advertising creates a desire for better clothing. Advertising creates a desire for a more attractive personal appearance. (not only . . . but also)

_____

_____

6. Newspapers and magazines are largely supported by advertising. Radio and television broadcasting* is largely supported by advertising. (just as)

_____

_____

7. Newspapers are important advertising media* because they reach millions of readers. Magazines are important advertising media because they reach millions of readers. (like)

_____

_____

PRACTICE: Sentences of Comparison

Write sentences of comparison using the given information.

1. The Japanese language/the Chinese language (similar to)

   The Japanese language is similar to the Chinese language.

2. Learning English (important/necessary)

   (not only . . . but also) _____

   _____

3. Physics/chemistry (interesting)

   (not only . . . but also) _____

   _____

---

broadcasting: sending out of radio and TV programs
media: systems of public communication—TV, radio, newspapers, etc. (singular: **medium**)

4. A working student/a nonworking student (busy)

(comparative form) _____

_____

5. Exercising daily/eating nutritious food (necessary for good health)

(similarly) _____

_____

6. My grandmother/my grandfather (active)

(not only . . . but also) _____

_____

7. Milk/cola drinks (good)

(comparative form) _____

8. Swimming/bicycling (fun)

(and . . . too) _____

_____

9. Rosa/I (tall)

(comparative form) _____

10. Rock music/music (popular)

(superlative form) _____

11. My present apartment/my old apartment (expensive)

(comparative form) _____

_____

Contrast Structure Words and Phrases

Now that you have learned to use comparison structure words and phrases to show how two things are the same, in this section you will learn to use contrast structure words and phrases to show how two things are different. These words and phrases connect the two parts of a contrast between two items, places, persons, and so on. The following table gives a partial list of the most common words and phrases that are used to show differences.

CONTRAST STRUCTURE WORDS AND PHRASES

Sentence Connectors	Conjunctions		Others
	Coordinating	**Subordinating**	
on the other hand	but	although even though	different from
in contrast			not like
	yet	while	
however		whereas	

Let's study each group of contrast structure words.

■ Sentence connectors are used to show a contrast between two complete sentences or independent clauses:

In contrast,

Independent clause.   *On the other hand,* + independent clause.

However,

Ryan loves rock music. However, Andrew loves jazz.

■ Subordinating conjunctions are used to show a contrast between two clauses, one independent and one dependent.
Remember that the dependent clause can come at the beginning or at the end of the sentence. If the dependent clause comes at the beginning, use a comma.

Use *although/even though* when the result in the independent clause is an unexpected surprise because of the information given in the dependent clause.

Even though I took the driving test three times, I couldn't pass it.
I couldn't pass the driving test although I took it three times.

Use *while/whereas* when the information in the first clause is in strong contrast (direct opposition) to the information in the second clause.

Some people like to exercise indoors, while others prefer the great outdoors*.
Whereas some people like to exercise indoors, others prefer the great outdoors.

Notice that a comma is placed after the independent clause before *while* or *whereas* to show strong contrast (direct opposition). This is an exception to the usual rule.

---

the great outdoors: another way to say **outdoors** (idiom)

■ Coordinating conjunctions are used to show a contrast between two independent clauses.

Use *but* when the information in the first independent clause is in complete contrast to the information in the second independent clause.
Independent clause, + *but* + independent clause.

I failed the driving test, but my best friend passed it.

Use *yet* when the result in the second independent clause is unexpected or a surprise because of the information in the first independent clause.
Independent clause, + *yet* + independent clause.

I failed the final examination, yet I passed the course.

NOTE: You can use *but* in place of *yet*:

I failed the final examination, but I passed the course.

■ Other contrast structure phrases are used to show a contrast between two people, things, and so on.
Subject + verb + different from + possessive.
                        (not like)
Subject + verb + different from + noun phrase.
                        (not like)

Ron's car is a silver sportscar.
Jeannie's car is a white station wagon.
    Ron's car is different from Jeannie's.
    Ron's car is not like Jeannie's.
    Watching a sporting event on television is different from (or is not like) seeing it in person.

PRACTICE: Using Contrast Words and Phrases

Write contrast sentences using the given information. Use a coordinator, a subordinator, and a sentence connector.

1. Jose swims well. Maria swims poorly.

   a. *Jose swims well, but Maria swims poorly.*

   b. *Jose swims well, whereas Maria swims poorly.*

   c. *Jose swims well. However, Maria swims poorly.*

2. Designer eyeglasses are attractive. I prefer contact lenses.

   a. _____

   b. _____

   c. _____

3. My apartment is large. Tanya's is small.

   a. _____

   b. _____

   c. _____

4. My roommate wants to go to the movies. Her boyfriend wants to go to a disco.

   a. _____

   b. _____

   c. _____

5. Fresh fruits and vegetables taste delicious. Canned fruits and vegetables are tasteless.

   a. _____

   b. _____

   c. _____

6. Dieting* and exercising will keep you in good health. Exercising by itself will not.

   a. _____

   b. _____

   c. _____

7. Jogging is boring. Playing tennis is exciting.

   a. _____

   b. _____

   c. _____

dieting: eating only nonfattening, healthy food; eating less in order to lose weight

8. Mark will go to college on a full scholarship. Carlos will have to work part-time.

    a. _____

    b. _____

    c. _____

9. In England, medical care is free. In the United States, people must pay for medical care.

    a. _____

    b. _____

    c. _____

PRACTICE: Contrast Sentences

A. Complete the following sentences. Punctuate correctly.

1. I love to go camping, but _my sister doesn't_____

2. Betty has gained ten pounds yet _____

_____

3. Although she should diet _____

_____

4. She should exercise although _____

_____

5. Fast food is not like _____

_____

6. _____ whereas Susan jogs every day.

7. Climbing mountains is great exercise   On the other hand _____

_____

8. I like to swim at the beach However _____

_____

9. Living on an island is different from _____

B. Write sentences showing differences between two places, people, or things. Use the contrast structure words in parentheses.

1. (but) _____

_____

2. (on the other hand) _____

_____

3. (while) _____

_____

4. (whereas) _____

_____

5. (different from) _____

_____

6. (however) _____

_____

7. (although) _____

_____

8. (not like) _____

_____

PREWRITING ACTIVITIES

Before you write a comparison and contrast composition, you should do some prewriting exercises just as you did in previous chapters. Remember that the first step is to brainstorm.

1. Decide on the two items or subjects you will compare.
2. Brainstorm for the similarities and differences of the items. When you are writing down your ideas, don't worry about separating the similarities from the differences. Just get your ideas down on paper. You can separate them later.

In the following example, the writer is going to point out the similarities and differences between two popular television shows.

Thesis statement:

The television shows "City Rackets" and "Private Eyes" are alike and yet different in several ways.

The writer makes a three-column list to brainstorm for similarities and differences between the two television shows:

Similarities and Differences	City Rackets	Private Eyes
take place in metropolitan cities	✓	✓
serious crimes of drugs, money, murder	✓	✓
main characters: a male and a female private detective		✓
local crime plots	✓	
local and international plots		✓
use of latest electronic equipment to capture criminals	✓	
lots of violence	✓	
some violence		✓
weekly show	✓	✓
big expensive cars		✓
many chase scenes	✓	
some chase scenes		✓
some comedy situations		✓
police involvement	✓	
guns	✓	
helicopters and boats to track criminals	✓	
boring dialogue	✓	
interesting dialogue		✓
main characters never in real danger		✓
always capture criminals	✓	

Now the writer crosses out unwanted points and makes a three-column list to separate the similarities from the differences.

	City Rackets	Private Eyes
I. Points of Similarity		
weekly shows	✓	✓
metropolitan city background	✓	✓
serious crimes about money, drugs, or murder	✓	✓
use of guns	✓	✓
fast action and chase scenes	✓	✓
criminals caught at end	✓	✓

	City Rackets	Private Eyes
II. Points of Difference		
main characters: two male undercover agents	✓	
main characters: a male and a female private detective		✓
local criminals	✓	
local and international criminals		✓
lots of violence	✓	
some violence		✓
guns always fired	✓	
guns seldom fired		✓
clever* dialogue		✓
boring dialogue	✓	
use of helicopters and boats in chase scenes	✓	
use of big, fancy cars		✓

These are the supporting points for the essay. The next step is to make a simple outline. Then, the writer can write the composition from the outline.

PRACTICE: Writing Comparison and Contrast Thesis Statements

Based on the given information, write a thesis statement that names the specific topics and the main ideas for a comparison and contrast composition.

1. (two professors) *My physics and chemistry professors have similar teaching methods, but their tests are very different.*

2. (two classes) _____

3. (two car models) _____

4. (two television shows) _____

clever: intelligent and funny

5. (two colleges/restaurants/night clubs) _____

_____

6. (high school/college) _____

_____

7. (two family members/friends) _____

_____

8. (your own topic) _____

_____

ON YOUR OWN!

A. Write a comparison and contrast composition in which you examine the similarities and differences between two items from the preceding practice on writing comparison and contrast thesis statements.

B. Go to a travel agency and get some brochures about two places in the United States or the world you would like to visit. Write a comparison and contrast composition about these places after you have done all the prewriting activities.

Hints for Success

- Do all the prewriting activities before you write your composition.
- Check your final draft against the essay checklist on page 102.

Index